The Studio

Life World Library
Life Nature Library
Time Reading Program
The Life History of the United States
Life Science Library
Great Ages of Man
Time-Life Library of Art
Time-Life Library of America
Foods of the World
This Fabulous Century
Life Library of Photography
The Time-Life Encyclopedia of Gardening

LIFE LIBRARY OF PHOTOGRAPHY

The Studio

BY THE EDITORS OF TIME-LIFE BOOKS

TIME-LIFE BOOKS, NEW YORK

ON THE COVER: Some basic equipment used by a professional studio photographer—flood and spot lamps at left, and a 4 x 5 view camera at right. The ground-glass viewing screen of the camera shows the inverted image of a still life—chessmen on a board—arranged on seamless paper and illuminated by the spot and the flood.

Contents

Portions of this book were written by Edmund White. Valuable assistance also was contributed by these individuals and departments of Time Inc.: Editorial Production, Robert W. Boyd Jr., Margaret T. Fischer; Editorial Reference, Peter Draz; Picture Collection, Doris O'Neil; TIME-LIFE News Service, Murray J. Gart; Correspondents Elisabeth Kraemer (Bonn), Margot Hapgood (London), Maria Vincenza Aloisi (Paris), Ann Natanson (Rome) and Sungyung Chang (Tokyo).

Photography can be approached from either of two directions. One approach is the way of the photojournalist, the quick-eyed observer who catches life on the wing as it flies past the camera lens, capturing the spontaneous picture that will make the front page—or the family album.

The studio photographer travels an entirely different route. A painstaking craftsman, he plans a picture as carefully as an architect designs a house, often taking days to arrange his composition and adjust his lighting before clicking his shutter. Rather than reporting events from the sidelines, he stages his own and exercises total control.

To acquire this control and increase his flexibility, the amateur beginning studio photography may wish to acquire a whole roomful of paraphernalia —floodlights, spotlights, reflectors, tripods, electronic-flash units and view cameras of various sizes. He may also wish, as professionals do, to operate like the designer of a theatrical production, constructing entire sets. Professional studios are sometimes large and elaborate, with barn-sized rooms, carloads of expensive equipment and big staffs of photo assistants, set builders, wardrobe mistresses and stylists. But an expensive establishment is really unnecessary for most studio work, and any amateur can set up his own studio with nothing more than a camera, a room, a few lights, and perhaps a roll of seamless photographic paper for a backdrop. And by borrowing a few techniques from professionals, he can even come close to their goal: a kind of photographic perfection reachable only through the studio photographer's unique ability to manipulate every step of the picture-taking process.

The Editors

EDWARD STEICHEN: *Self-Portrait with Photographic Paraphernalia*, 1929

Making, Not Taking, Pictures

Studio photographers are among the highest-paid, most influential figures in the entire field of photography. When such magazines as *Vogue* or *Harper's Bazaar* publish an important studio photographer's pictures, his personal taste may start an important trend in the fashion industry, a major business in the United States. In his advertising photographs—and studio photographers do their most lucrative work for Madison Avenue—his success or failure can affect the fortunes of the product or service he is helping to sell. If he does portraits of celebrities, his view of an individual not only may become the public's most enduring image of that person, but also may subtly change the way we look at ourselves—as a woman may more or less consciously adopt the image of a currently popular fashion model. And his shots of still lifes may convey an artistic beauty that measurably heightens the esthetics of photography. Not that all studio photographers inhabit such a rarefied atmosphere. Many work from quiet neighborhood studios where they record the events close to the hearts of their clients—weddings, birthdays, christenings, bar mitzvahs, promotions or just plain family portraits.

Varied as the products of their work may be, all studio photographers share a common distinction: the total control that each one exercises, for better or worse, over his picture. He stages his shot, creates it to suit his preconceived notion of what it should be. There are few if any lucky "accidents" in studio photography. The photographer arranges every element as much as is humanly possible. He poses his sitters or models, places the props, frames the setting, ordains the camera angle and use of lights. To achieve desired color tones he uses filters and to attain a desired mood he may deliberately blur his film, even shake his camera. The studio photographer is the general so confident of his battle plan that once it is completed the actual pushing of the shutter button is often done by a subordinate.

As the name implies, studio photography was born and raised in the studio. Working at first with the available light coming through the studio skylights and later with increasingly sophisticated artificial light sources the photographer maintained complete control, ultimately in any kind of weather. Usually working with a view camera *(Chapter 5),* the studio photographer took portraits, group pictures and an occasional still life. But today studio photography has a paradoxical dimension. No longer is it confined to the studio itself: photographers transport their studios outdoors, and the whole world has become their stage. Using their own lights, backdrops, props, models and a wide variety of cameras—still including the view camera—studio photographers do not usually travel light. The celebrated studio photographer Irving Penn takes along five cameras, two sets of auxiliary lenses and 15 pieces of luggage on his frequent worldwide tours. With studio photographers the studio goes wherever they go.

Perhaps the most concise definition of studio photography was delivered by one of the finest portrait photographers in the business, Philippe Halsman: "*making,* not taking a picture." No disparagement of picture "takers" was intended. The French master-photographer Henri Cartier-Bresson, for one, *takes* pictures. According to Halsman, Cartier-Bresson "never interferes in the action he photographs and his unobtrusiveness is so unique that it has created the legend that, at the moment of picture taking, Cartier becomes invisible." No one could ever accuse the studio photographer of being invisible. He is everywhere, imposing his will upon the picture. While photographers like Cartier-Bresson steal scenes from the life that swirls around them, the studio photographer consciously creates his scenes to suit the image already in his mind's eye.

Among the picturemakers are many expert craftsmen, each with his special view of the world. But two studio photographers—Richard Avedon and Penn—are generally recognized as the most versatile, creative and individualistic forces in the field. No two modern practitioners are more widely imitated—the ultimate compliment from their fellow photographers. Yet imitations have seldom been successful, for the personalities of Avedon and Penn infuse all their work. Both men burst onto the scene in the years following World War II and quickly established themselves in three phases of studio photography—portraiture, fashion and advertising. And Penn eventually extended his mastery into the fourth phase—still-life photography. Their commercial photography, particularly advertising, made them well-to-do. Their portraits established their credentials as men of uncommon insight into the nature of humans.

Avedon brought to studio photography a restless, romantic style—really a series of styles, since his pictures reflect many attitudes and moods. He started as a fashion photographer, and the picture that revealed his flair for the unusual was shot in 1950. It showed one of the leading models of the day, Dorian Leigh, laughing as she threw her arms around the winner of a bicycle race in France. It caused an uproar in the fashion business—it was not the custom to show a model in such a human act. Avedon went on from there, bringing new sensations—even humor—into fashion. He put a model on roller skates and sent her cruising down the streets of Paris. He placed one girl among a herd of wild-eyed elephants; and on other assignments showed the model sobbing or smiling at her husband or pushing a baby carriage. Once the shock of such natural credible pictures was absorbed by the fashion world, "togetherness" fashion and advertising shots found a popularity that lingered into the 1970s.

Avedon's style has been mirrored in the pert faces of his models, from Dorian Leigh and her younger sister Suzy Parker to the English model Jean

Shrimpton and the young, waiflike girl of the late 1960s, Penelope Tree. But the girls are never simply pretty faces to Avedon. He spends a great deal of time talking to them, getting them in the mood for the picture-taking session. He even plays their favorite songs on his studio hi-fi and, when the occasion demands, offers coffee or Cokes. He realizes that models live in the rushed, highly stylized, somewhat unreal world of beautiful clothes and perpetual elegance, which can inspire many psychological problems. He once described models as "a group of underdeveloped, frightened, insecure women, most of whom have been thought ugly as children—too tall and too skinny. They are all subject to trauma where their looks are concerned. You have to make them *feel* beautiful."

Clearly, his involvement with his models is deep. He once said, "I have to be a little bit in love with my models." But on another occasion, when asked about the nature of this love, he explained it in less romantic terms: "It's like the feeling you have for kittens or puppies."

Nevertheless, Avedon's first wife was one of his models. She was Dorcas Nowell, known professionally as Doe Avedon, and he loved to photograph her—a busman's holiday for a studio photographer. The marriage lasted five years; in 1951 he married again, the former Evelyn Franklin, a handsome woman determinedly unconnected with the fashion world. (She even refuses to let her husband take informal pictures of her.) The couple live in a town house in New York City with their teen-age son, John. Avedon, who rarely drinks and doesn't smoke, seldom goes to parties and prefers quiet nights at home. His energy is reserved for his assignments, which have in the past kept him working from dawn to late into the evening. He varies his equipment with the job, sometimes using a simple Rolleiflex for photographing the entire collection of a prestigious Parisian designer, but at times has hired generator trucks to light up a whole street to show off a dress collection, with Parisian policemen employed to hold back the curious crowds.

Avedon's energy and probing vision, so graphically displayed in his fashion and commercial photography, extend significantly into his portraiture. His skill and insight have drawn hundreds of people to his studios, including many of the world's most famous people. So great is his reputation that for private sittings, rarely held these days, Avedon charges $1,500. In return the sitter receives a single print.

Like all studio photographers, Avedon jealously guards his independence and his right to control everything in his pictures. When he was still a comparatively unknown photographer, LIFE commissioned him to shoot a series of pictures of New York City. Knowing that such a story could immeasurably enhance his career, he accepted the assignment—but found he could not complete it. "The trouble was that when I got out into the street," he explained, "I didn't like invading the privacy of perfect strangers. It seemed such an aggressive thing to do. Also, I have to control what I shoot, and I found that I couldn't control Times Square." His refuge was the studio. "I always prefer to work in the studio," he has said. "It isolates people from their environment. They become, in a sense, symbolic of themselves. I often feel that people come to me to be photographed as they would go to a doctor or a fortuneteller—to find out how they are . . . I have to engage them. Otherwise there's nothing to photograph. The concentration has to come from me and involve them. Sometimes the force of it grows so strong that sounds in the studio go unheard. Time stops. We share a brief, intense intimacy. But it's unearned. It has no past, no future."

This last wistful, almost rueful note, is sounded by many leading studio photographers. With loving care and fierce intensity, a man like Avedon creates a scene suitable for photographing. He fixes and fidgets until every material object is exactly right. He talks to the model or sitter, learning to understand the person, trying to grasp the elusive strands of personality. Through this long, laborious approach, a specific moment is created. For a brief instant the look of the subject, backed by the props and setting, tells the story. The shutter button is pushed and the picture preserves the moment. But it is fleeting. The subject's attitude changes, the mood evaporates, the luminosity fades. The letdown often brings a sense of loss to both parties —but if all has gone well, a picture worthy of it all is there.

Do men seek out studio photography, or do they just drift into it? Avedon seemed to drift into it, although perhaps through unconscious design. He wanted to be a poet, but when he dropped out of a Bronx high school at 17 he got a job as an errand boy at a small photography concern. He enlisted in the Merchant Marine in 1942 after the start of World War II and as a going-away present his father, who operated a women's-wear shop, gave him a Rolleiflex camera. With camera in hand, Avedon applied for a job in the photography branch of the service and spent the war years in Sheepshead Bay in Brooklyn taking identification pictures of Merchant Marine personnel. In his spare time he took more demanding pictures and when he left the service landed a job photographing models at Bonwit Teller, the New York specialty store. He had always been aware of fashion photography; thanks to his father's business, he had grown up with fashion magazines around the house and had even kept a scrapbook of the pictures he liked in them. After a year at Bonwit's, he decided to move on. He put together a portfolio of his best work —along with some of his spare-time Merchant Marine photos—and applied for a job at *Harper's Bazaar*.

The art director of *Bazaar* at that time (the mid-1940s) was a man who would exert a profound influence over the direction of modern fashion photography; he once taught Irving Penn, he discovered Avedon and later he worked with Avedon's protégé Hiro, one of studio photography's biggest names today. His name is Alexey Brodovitch, a Russian immigrant whose life story would test the imagination of a Hollywood screenwriter. The artistically talented son of a prosperous doctor, Brodovitch ran away from home while still a teenager, first to fight with the Russian Army in World War I, then to battle with the White Army against the Bolsheviks after the revolution in 1917. Severely wounded in a Red Army artillery bombardment, he managed to escape first to Constantinople, then to France. Recovered from his injuries, Brodovitch found a job in Paris painting scenery for the exiled Ballet Russe, which was then under the direction of the legendary Sergei Diaghilev. In 1925, after winning first prize in a Parisian poster-design contest and gold medals at the International Exhibition of Decorative Arts, Brodovitch turned his hand to advertising. Three years later his reputation was good enough for the Philadelphia Museum of Art to invite him to establish advertising classes in a school of industrial art. He moved to America and in 1934 was named art director of *Harper's Bazaar,* a position he held until 1958.

Brodovitch was more than a trained artist; he had the gift for aphorisms that contained worthwhile lessons for any serious student of photography. "Start working without a camera," he once said. "Cut out a window in a piece of cardboard and observe, discover and decide what to snap." Perhaps most important to a young photographer like Avedon was this advice: "Develop a statement of your own. Shout, don't whisper." When Avedon presented Brodovitch his portfolio, the art director was impressed by a picture snapped during Avedon's Merchant Marine hitch, a slightly out-of-focus study of two brothers. In that blurred photograph Brodovitch saw something that appealed to his romantic nature—Avedon had caught the sense of people actually moving, not frozen for the lens. Avedon was hired for his "mistake," a blurred picture. It would lead him into a new, poetic world, and the arresting work he began to turn out, subjective and suggestive of more than the prints showed, gave studio photography a creative push forward.

Today, Avedon regularly contributes signed editorial work to *Vogue,* having left *Harper's Bazaar* in 1965. He also turns out an impressive number of unsigned beauty advertisements. The editorial work provides him with prestige, the advertisements with a great deal of money. Over the years he has compiled scores of portraits of famous sitters and in the summer of 1970 a large selection of these pictures was exhibited in Minneapolis at the Institute of Arts. The studies ranged from the Duke and Duchess of Windsor, Marian Anderson and the late American Nazi Party leader George Lincoln Rockwell, to the seven defendants in the 1969 Chicago conspiracy trial. Critics were not unanimous in their praise for the work. According to *The New York*

Times, most of Avedon's portraits were harsh and unflattering, not at all like his lovely likenesses of fashion models. His picture of the Windsors, for instance, showed them as "haggard with guilt and dissipation." Avedon parries such charges. The lines, smiles and weathered eyes of his celebrated sitters he regards as "sermons on bravado."

In contrast to the romantic vivacity of Avedon's photography, the work of Irving Penn is suffused with a cool, introspective beauty. His tranquillity and urbanity are beautifully expressed in a photograph of a stylish model picking a piece of tobacco from her tongue with a perfectly manicured nail, or a shot of the contents spilled from a woman's handbag: a gold pill case, scattered tranquilizers, a cigarette holder, a pencil for jotting down appointments. His clinical view stays with him whether shooting painstakingly preened high-fashion models in New York or traveling to distant corners of the globe on editorial assignments for *Vogue.* At least once a year Penn sets out to explore new territory—Nepal, New Guinea, Peru, Dahomey—searching for new and arresting people—and faces—to shoot. Wherever he goes, he usually takes with him a portable studio. Instead of catching New Guinea highlanders, for example, in their huts, Penn carefully poses the people he visits inside his traveling studio *(pages 98-102).* As he explains it, "I'm not a photojournalist and am not especially interested in the kind of photographs that result from showing people in their natural surroundings. I suspect that when a stranger pokes a camera at them, they become *not* as they really are. Therefore, I prefer to use a neutral environment—a photographic studio or its equivalent. Here the subject and I relate more easily to each other as one human being to another rather than as a tourist to a native, let us say. Also, in a studio, I'm able to control the posing, the play of light and shadow, and thus to enjoy the photographic subtleties that mean so much to me. This *is* photography for me. . . ."

Frank, intent, deceptively shy with an iron will, Penn, like Avedon, became a photographer almost by accident. Born in Plainfield, New Jersey, he studied design under Brodovitch at the Philadelphia Museum School of Art. But after a few odd jobs in New York, he fled to Mexico to do what he had dreamed of doing—become a painter. For a year he toiled in the bleak volcanic desert called the Pedregal in the Federal District, but the results were far from what he expected. He came to the depressing realization that as a painter he would never be more than simply mediocre. Penn's deep strain of self-awareness and practicality helped him make the important decision to give up. It is also reflected in the way he destroyed his paintings: he simply dropped them into a bathtub and scrubbed the paint from them. Later he used the fine linen canvases as tablecloths.

Returning to New York City in 1943, Penn took a job in the *Vogue* art department after showing the magazine's new art director, Alexander Liberman, some drawings and a few snapshots of fruit and scrubbed graffiti. Penn's job was to suggest covers for the *Vogue* photographers, and most of the suggestions were rejected; the photographers wanted to think up their own covers. Before long, Liberman proposed that Penn shoot covers himself and Penn did—his first one being done with a borrowed camera. The picture was a stark, eye-stopping still life of a brown leather bag, a scarf and gloves, some lemons and oranges and a huge topaz. It appeared on the cover October 1, 1943, the first of nearly 150 covers he would do for *Vogue.*

Penn joined the American Field Service in 1944 and served on ambulance duty with the British army in Italy and India. When he returned to *Vogue* after the war, he embarked on a series of stunning portraits, including studies of Picasso, Colette, the American artist John Marin and the distinguished jurist Learned Hand. On assignment, he also took a charming series of pictures of tradesmen and everyday workers—postmen, chauffeurs, plumbers—shot in New York, Paris and London.

Through the years, Penn's innovations—an austere, uncluttered style and a restless urge to take his brand of studio photography out into the exotic corners of the world—have been so influential and so widely imitated that today few photographers even realize that the ideas they are copying originated with him. He was also a pioneer in the use of color film, yet Penn has said, "I think that black-and-white pictures are intrinsically finer than color. I think I have never seen a really *great* color photograph. When I think of great photographs I immediately think of black and white."

Penn's portraits of celebrities are among his most famous black-and-white pictures. Often he shoots the seated half-figures, cropping the head on his ground-glass screen to "create a disturbing tension." For a brief period, he also devised a wide variety of compositions by placing the sitter in a corner. Although these eccentric ways of picturing his subjects have attracted many imitators, Penn explains that he originally stuck his celebrities in corners because he didn't "feel able to cope with them. You see, I used the corner as a prop for myself, as a protection, but I found later that by simply taking subjects out of their normal circumstances I made the problem easier too. By putting them in my studio they had less to depend on in holding onto their public façades." Once the façade has dropped and Penn has taken the portrait, a few of his famous sitters end up intensely disliking the picture. "No subject minds a boring picture," Penn summarizes. "They mind a picture that has gotten to the soft core."

Penn, whose brother Arthur is the theater and motion-picture director, is married to one of the most frequently photographed models of all time, Lisa

Fonssagrives. A Swedish beauty whose handsomely sculpted features are the personification of sophisticated charm, Mrs. Penn was a frequent model in Penn photographs. The couple and their teen-age son Tom (her daughter by a previous marriage, Mia, is a fashion designer) live in New York City and on a Long Island farm where they once bred Cheviot sheep. In the summer they travel to Sweden, to cruise on a sailboat they maintain on the fjord where Mrs. Penn was born and where they have built a house.

In his work and life, Penn reflects his credo: show "the very still, the very quiet." His studio in New York is subdued and spare. The walls, floors and cabinets are all painted gray, a neutral tone that works to the distinct advantage of sitters. Photography is a business as well as a passion to Penn; he employs four assistants, a secretary-manager, and part-time bookkeepers, accountants, lawyers and a maintenance service. With assistants to do the menial tasks, Penn never puts his hands in the developer and has not changed film in a camera for 20 years.

This efficient organization frees Penn for his task of making pictures, which he sets about with near-frightening dedication. During a portrait sitting, a reverential hush falls over the studio. Conversations are minimal, instructions are issued in whispers, the phones are cut off. The silence begets some tension and more than one sitter has felt overwhelmed by it. Only the clicking of the shutter breaks the silence. The tension is not relieved until Penn has the picture he feels he wants.

As with Penn and Avedon, the dedication of the studio photographers is great. They alone make the picture and control it, starting from scratch. The results from the top professionals are sometimes spectacular, always perceptive, as the gallery of pictures on the following pages shows.

The Craft of Portraiture

YOUSUF KARSH: *John L. Lewis*, 1944

By his insistence on total control over his works, the studio photographer limits himself to pictures of people and things in a delimited setting. But the restriction is not as confining as it seems, for his subjects are as varied as portraits, pets, dresses, cars and almost every commercial product made. Of these the most common is the portrait.

Two of the finest practitioners, Yousuf Karsh of Ottawa and Arnold Newman of New York, both do extensive research on each sitter to learn how to reveal his character. But it needed no research for Karsh to know that the longtime head of the United Mine Workers of America, John L. Lewis *(left)*, was a crusty, strong-willed man. Lewis substantiated this reputation at once. Striding into his Washington office after Karsh had set up his lights, Lewis sat before the camera with his hat still on, glowered and ordered, "Shoot!" Karsh soothed Lewis into removing his hat and relaxing somewhat. But the roughhewn nature of the former coal miner is stamped on the portrait.

Newman had an easier time with the Japanese sculptor-architect Isamu Noguchi. He trained his 4 x 5 view camera on his subject's upper torso to make the head and body seem part of an abstract work by the sculptor. Newman frequently uses background props related to his subjects and makes long exposures (of a second or more) to permit small apertures that give great depth of field, bringing a close association between man and prop. His subjects rarely move and blur the pictures, for he talks until he puts them at ease. How does he know when a subject is at ease? "When a kind of sleepiness overcomes him," Newman explains.

ARNOLD NEWMAN: *Isamu Noguchi*, 1947

21

The commercial photographers who make formal portraits of recently promoted executives, of brides, of children on graduation day, probably outnumber all other practitioners of the craft. Their task is not to seek out the subtle nuances of a complex personality, but to present their subjects in a strong and flattering light.

Perhaps no man wants his affirmative qualities to show through a formal portrait more than a head of state does. As the portraits at right attest, the firm of Harris & Ewing, Washington photographers of American Presidents since 1905, has a clear understanding of its responsibility to them.

When Harris & Ewing opened for business the capital had no major studio capable of making—for supplying to news agencies—distinguished-looking portraits of its leading citizens: Presidents, Cabinet members, Senators, Congressmen, Supreme Court justices. So George W. Harris and Mrs. Martha Ewing, who were old friends from California, set out to fill the gap. Their first portrait of a President was made midway in Theodore Roosevelt's term of office. Harris once recalled T.R. as "probably the most dynamic man I ever photographed. William Howard Taft was probably the jolliest." As might be expected, Calvin Coolidge was the most casual. He strolled over to the studio for his sitting; all the others were photographed in the White House.

Theodore Roosevelt

William Howard Taft

Woodrow Wilson

Warren G. Harding

Calvin Coolidge

Herbert Hoover

Franklin D. Roosevelt

Harry S. Truman

Dwight D. Eisenhower

John F. Kennedy

In making these two images of Sophia Loren, placed together to create a multiple portrait, Richard Avedon purposely blurred the images to achieve a romantic effect. The wind-tossed hair, closed or lowered eyelids and imprecise facial characteristics all contribute a sensuous dimension that a sharper picture might have lost.

Avedon achieves such an expressive quality by an approach that might seem self-defeating. "My photographs don't go below the surface," he has stated. "They're readings of what's on the surface. I have great faith in surfaces. A good one is full of clues. But whenever I become absorbed in the beauty of a face, in the excellence of a single feature, I feel I've lost what's really there."

To make this romanticized dual portrait of Sophia Loren, Richard Avedon used a Rolleiflex with strobe attachment. He achieved the wind-whipped look by having Miss Loren bend her head forward, then toss it back as an electric fan sent a breeze through her hair. She repeated this motion about 50 times as Avedon froze the movement with the strobe. From all his shots, these two were pasted together in a photomontage, which was rephotographed to make a negative for prints.

RICHARD AVEDON: *Sophia Loren*, 1970

RODDY McDOWALL: *Birgit Nilsson*, 1966

Some of the most successful portraits of celebrities are made by photographers who have an intimate knowledge of the entertainment world. Roddy McDowall, who made the portrait of opera soprano Birgit Nilsson above, was a child movie star in England; he grew up to become an actor and film director. His ability to convey the characteristics and personality of performers often springs from his friendships with them.

He has said that actors, like children and pets, photograph best when they are in a familiar setting—playing a role in which they are at ease.

Barbara Morgan, in making a series of portraits of the eminent dancer Martha Graham *(opposite),* watched performances and studied the dance for five years. Her pictures were not taken during performances but came from studio sessions with Miss Graham.

So shy of the camera is opera star Birgit Nilsson that to make this portrait Roddy McDowall decided to catch her reflection in a dressing-room mirror so that she would not tense up facing a lens. He used the lens-shift adjustment on his view camera (Chapter 5) to avoid picking up its reflection along with Miss Nilsson's.

In an acrobatically graceful motion, Martha ▶ Graham portrays a tragic moment from a dance. Her body merges horizontally with a black band on the studio wall, but her arched left leg and full, sweeping skirt provide an uplifting sense of motion. The picture was made with a 4 x 5 Speed Graphic at 1/800 second, using multiple flash.

26

BARBARA MORGAN: *Martha Graham in "Letter to the World,"* 1940

Making a portrait is never simple, since there are so many variables to take into account—but sometimes a photographer wants to make extra trouble for himself. A good example is Philippe Halsman's famous portrait of the eccentric surrealist artist Salvador Dali *(opposite).* The picture was so complicated it took 26 attempts to get; some of the noble failures are seen at right. The inspiration for the photograph was a painting by Dali (on the large easel) of the Greek legend of Leda and the swan. Everything in the painting, which shows Zeus approaching Leda in the form of a swan, hangs in space in accordance with Dali's perception of the world as one great conglomeration of atoms, each hovering around its nucleus.

Halsman and the artist, who are old friends, mulled over a lot of ideas for a photograph that would dramatically display Dali in his suspended world. Dali even suggested stuffing a duck with dynamite and exploding it as he jumped at his easel. Halsman vetoed that plan as dangerous, cruel and probably illegal. In time it was resolved that cats and water, hanging in space as Dali leaped in the background, would convey the desired surrealist mood. The easels were suspended by wires from the studio ceiling and Mrs. Halsman held the chair aloft. Three assistants threw the cats from right to left while another hurled water out of a bucket from the opposite direction. The entire shooting took about six hours. At the picture session, Dali jumped at a blank easel. On the print of the last shot *(opposite),* he painted on the blank easel a fitting subject—a person suffering through a feline nightmare.

First try: Dali doesn't get off the ground.

Now the cats are hardly in the picture.

Cats okay, but water obscures Dali's face.

One cat showing—two cats missing.

Fine—except a secretary accidentally walks by.

Now the chair hides Dali's face.

PHILIPPE HALSMAN: *Dalí Atomicus*, 1948

Fashions Indoors and Out

MELVIN SOKOLSKY: *Suspended Model*, 1962

Few studio photographers have greater need of inventiveness than those who picture fashions. To catch the viewer's eye and instantly convey the idea of desirability, the fashion photographer will stretch his control over his pictures to its limits. He may build a mood with precise use of lighting *(opposite)*—or create a fresh world of fantasy *(left)*. When photographing the new collections of clothing designed in Paris, he may pose beautifully turned-out models atop the Eiffel Tower or stand them rakishly on bridge railings over the Seine (a few have fallen in as the result of some photographer's zeal for an unusual angle), or seal off a whole block to keep away traffic that would destroy his illusion. For wherever his studio is, at home or on a city street, he must conjure the elusive atmosphere of high fashion.

To make pictures that would bring attention to a new fashion line, photographer Melvin Sokolsky had an aluminum-framed plastic bubble made in New York. After it was tested by being dangled over the Palisades cliffs in New Jersey, the bubble was flown to Paris where—with a model inside—it was suspended at various picturesque sites from a crane. Here the bubble hangs in St. Germain-en-Laye, a Paris suburb.

*A lighting scheme was tailor-made to show off ►
this gown by emphasizing the contrast between the slim, clinging gown and its huge, billowing sleeves. Only one light source was used—an electronic flash bounced off an umbrella reflector. Illuminating the model from the side, it made a picture that transcends fashion to become a stately study of the human form.*

GUY BOURDIN: *Classic Gown*, 1970

The Portrait of a Pet

YLLA: *Chinchilla Cat,* 1952

Studio portraits of pets are made with some of the same care and attention that are lavished on high-fashion models. Many pet portraits are of course simply treasured mementos of the family cat or dog. In the case of show animals, however, money may be involved, for the pictures are often used to sell the pups of a prize litter or to exhibit a champion standing at stud.

The restlessness of many animals makes them difficult as portrait subjects, and to avoid blurred pictures photographers generally use strobe lights and fast shutter speeds as well as tricks to hold the subject's attention.

To fix this chinchilla cat's attention and get her walking, her kitten was taken across the studio and held by an assistant. Electronic flash highlighted the animal's fur and froze her motion.

This portrait of a champion Afghan was made as if ▶ the sitter were human. Before the photographer started shooting, he spent 45 minutes talking to the dog to help it get accustomed to the studio surroundings and assume its relaxed pose.

NORMAN WIGHTMAN: *Afghan "Shah,"* 1970

Catching the Charm of a Child

IRVING PENN: *A Florentine Child, Elisabetta Cristina Giuffrida-Ruggeri, 1948*

More and more the studio photographer has moved away from the stiffly posed, self-conscious pictures of children so favored for decades by Main Street studio craftsmen. Instead, the modern studio photographer tries to show the essence of the child's nature by allowing him to act out fantasy games *(opposite)* or by encouraging the child to strike stylized poses *(left)*.

Since a relaxed atmosphere brings out the best in children, studio portraits are often made at home or in familiar surroundings. The trick is to get the child to reveal through his expression the wonders that he contemplates. With patience, a low-key approach and soft lighting that does not disturb the child, the studio photographer creates pictures that reflect the glow of childhood.

A pose and mood reminiscent of Renaissance portraits characterize this study of a little Italian girl at her home in Florence. One of a series on Italians done for Vogue after World War II, the picture captures in its quiet charm the timeless innocence of children the world over.

Three of the 34 great-grandchildren of the distinguished American architect Stanford White pose in period clothes in an ornate hall of White's Long Island estate. The comfort of the familiar house and the fun of trying on costumes enabled the children to radiate the sense of pleasure that infuses the picture, which was made in sunlight bounced from an adjoining porch.

TONI FRISSELL: *Costume Trunk*, 1964

Art for Advertising's Sake

MILTON HALBERSTADT: *Still Life with Tomatoes, 1962*

The making of an expert still life demands close adherence to the basic rules of studio photography: pay keen attention to detail, arrange objects with concern for composition and, above all, take maximum pains with lighting.

Since most still lifes are now made for commercial purposes, they challenge the studio photographer to find esthetic values in the humblest of utilitarian objects *(left)*. But sometimes a commercial assignment inspires art for art's sake. The picture on the opposite page was the result of a sudden inspiration that came to photographer Nob Fukuda in his Osaka studio while he was making some photographs of small kitchen appliances. He removed them from his table and replaced them with these items: a framed reproduction of a painting by the 19th Century French artist Henri Rousseau, several hemp palm leaves in a vase and four eggs. Given the proper lighting, the ingredients formed a still life of simple dignity.

This still life, made as an advertisement for tomato paste, shows a halved tomato near a bell jar containing other pieces of the fruit. In the background is a jar of water with sprigs of fennel, an herb used in making the paste. Light comes from a specially designed fixture—a 10-foot-high parabolic apparatus using five bulbs of 500 watts each—that shows the succulence of the fruit.

To bring out the interplay of light, shadow and ▶ color in this serene still life, three light sources were used. One 500-watt bulb was placed in the overhead fixture. Another 500-watt bulb went into a flood lamp on the right, diffused through translucent paper. A 1,000-watt spot was played on the table to convey the shape of the eggs.

NOB FUKUDA: *Still Life*, 1970

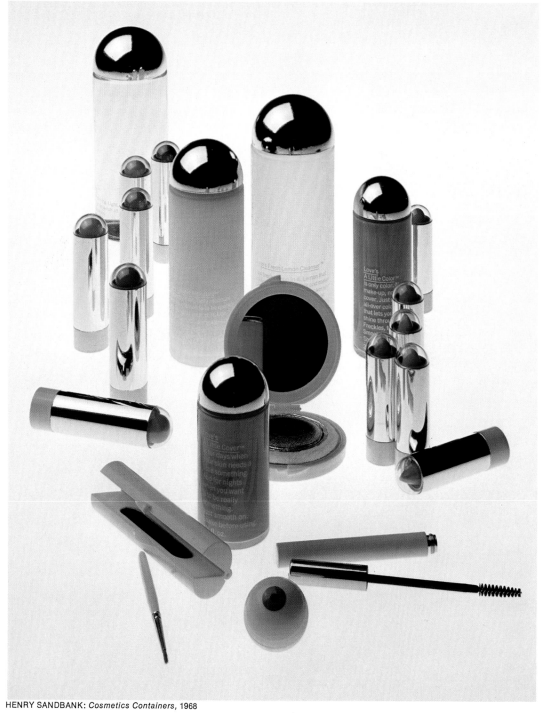

HENRY SANDBANK: *Cosmetics Containers,* 1968

In the 19th Century commercial enterprises relied entirely on art work for their advertisements and promotional publications. Today they go primarily to the studio photographer, whose camera is used to stimulate buyer interest in everything from sewing accessories *(opposite)* to automobiles *(overleaf).*

Often the public attitude toward a product or service—the image, both literal and figurative—is determined by photographs. Indeed, photographers are sometimes called in as consultants when a new line is to be promoted. This was the case when Love Cosmetics decided to market some of its products in futuristic package designs. The photographer, Henry Sandbank, worked closely with the packaging designer and advertising art director as they developed a cosmetic line that would appeal to young women who grew up in the space age. Sandbank then created a series of pictures, one of which is at left, emphasizing the glistening metallic look of the new products.

The cylindrical, modernistic cast of these cosmetics containers was emphasized by placing them on a large sheet of Plexiglass and lighting from below with two 500-watt floodlights. A 750-watt spotlight trained on them from above introduced highlights on the burnished surfaces.

To emphasize the slate coloring of the zipper ▶ and seam binding in this advertising picture for sewing accessories, Peter Scolamiero bought a piece of slate and spread the articles on it. To soften the picture, he employed two 1,000-watt lights diffused through a sheet of opal glass.

PETER SCOLAMIERO: *Notions on Slate*, 1968

ERNST HAAS: *Volkswagen in New Mexico,* 1964

Studio photographers, along with automobile stylists, long ago began capitalizing on the fact that to many people a car is more than a means of transportation; it is also a status symbol, a member of the family—and a functional triumph of modern technology. The photographers' job was to heighten this complex of feelings, thus increasing pride of ownership—and sales. As a result, automobiles have been photographed in every exotic—and familiar —corner of the globe.

Ernst Haas took his handsome mood shot for Volkswagen using an adobe church in New Mexico as a backdrop connoting strength and durability *(left);* Hiro, on location in California *(opposite),* viewed the Mercury as a machine with a unique place of its own in society —and he decided to make a portrait, not merely a picture. To convey the sense of life, he strategically placed three lights: one in the interior to "wake it up," another under the front grill "to lift it off the ground," and the third aimed at the front to bring out the contours. He also opened the doors, suggesting that the automobile possesses wings or even open arms. ☐

The photographer was in Taos, New Mexico when this picture came to him. With the sun's rays casting a shadow of the car on the adobe wall of a church, he composed his photograph to relate a durable product of mass production to an example of timeless craftsmanship.

For this new-model portrait of a metallic brown ▶ sedan, Hiro placed the automobile on a promontory at Big Sur, California. Shooting on a hazy mid-morning with strobe lights and infrared film, he experimented with some 20 different combinations of filters, putting three and four of them onto his camera at a time, until he achieved this unusual vision of sleek, animated power.

When Burlington Industries asked Lionel
Freedman for a picture that would show all
the company's fabrics at once, he went to work on
this room setting in his large New York studio
(pages 64-67). No real room would ever contain
such a wide range of fabrics, so he decided
to build a surreal room of his own imagining. He
gave the picture a dreamlike quality by using
indirect lighting and by draping long strips from
bolts of cloth across the highly polished
floor. At the sides of the room, fabrics are
gathered in hangings, as a utilitarian
counterpoint to the wandering strips at center.

LIONEL FREEDMAN: *Fabric Display,* 1960

Evolution of the Studio 2

Techniques Past and Present 46

A thriving 19th Century studio, the establishment ▶
of Henry Holler in Brooklyn, New York, is shown
opposite in an 1891 engraving. Used as a
trademark, it was printed on cardboard mountings
that the studio supplied with its pictures. The
large radial sign, oversized wall lettering and the
prideful claim to being an "art gallery" all
indicate the imposing place the photographic
studio had in the commercial life of the city.

Techniques Past and Present

From the very beginning, photography has been a studio art. The oldest surviving daguerreotype, made by Louis Daguerre in 1837, is a still life with plaster cupids and a wine bottle artfully arranged in a corner of the inventor's studio. An impressionistic murkiness pervades the picture, the result of dim interior lighting and the slow reaction time of the first cameras and plates. Nonetheless it is an admirable example of studio photography.

One of the first to be impressed was the American inventor Samuel F. B. Morse. He met Daguerre in Paris in 1839 and was so enthralled by the Frenchman's studio interiors that he declared them to be "Rembrandt perfected." He resolved to bring Daguerre's process to America, and in doing so, opened up one of this country's first photography studios.

Morse's principal interest was in making portraits. Besides being the inventor of the telegraph, he was one of the nation's leading portrait painters, and professor of art at New York University. Photography fascinated him because it promised to be a fast and accurate way to make portrait studies for his canvases. With a chemistry professor at N.Y.U., John W. Draper, who was interested in the scientific problems of photography, Morse built a glassed-in studio on the roof of the university building in 1840. Shortly afterward he opened a second studio, a veritable "palace for the sun," on the top floor of a nearby commercial building, and went into business, taking daguerreotype portraits and teaching photography, while waiting for the United States government to grant him recognition and money for his telegraph.

Like Morse, almost all the early studio photographers were portraitists. And all of them faced the same perplexing problem: how to bring enough light into the studio to make an exposure. Indoor exposure times for the early daguerreotypes were so protracted—a half hour or more—that portrait photography seemed at first impossible. How could any sitter keep still for so long a period? Daguerre himself said it could never be done, but inventive photographers were already working out ways to reduce exposure times by using faster lenses and concentrated light sources. Strong light, in fact, was a prerequisite. Most portrait photographers, like Morse, solved the lighting problem by building studios with glass roofs and directing the exterior light onto the subject's face with mirrors. There were some ingenious variations on this basic scheme. Alexander S. Wolcott, who opened a studio on New York's Broadway in March 1840, several months before Morse opened his, brought in sunlight through the window. He used a system of gigantic reflectors cantilevered over the sidewalk to catch the sun's rays and focus them onto the subject. To protect the sitter's eyes from glare, the light was filtered through a rack of glass bottles filled with blue dye.

Daguerreotype portrait studios were an immediate popular success. Everyone wanted his features immortalized by this miraculous new process.

"Daguerrean galleries," as they were called, sprang up in every city. By 1853 there were 86 in New York City alone, and an estimated 1,000 New Yorkers made their living by working in them. The Commonwealth of Massachusetts reported in 1855 that it had 134 professional daguerreotype artists, and that during the year they had made 403,626 pictures. The studios ranged from rudimentary to lavish. In frontier communities in the West, the local photographer might set up his camera in a single room over the barber shop. Some big-city daguerreotype studios were as richly appointed as opera houses, with commodious waiting rooms, an abundance of side rooms where the portraits were taken and labs where they were developed. One of the most fashionable was opened by Mathew B. Brady, later of Civil War fame, in New York in 1853. It profoundly impressed the reporter from Humphrey's *Daguerrean Journal,* who wrote: "The walls are covered with satin and gold paper. The ceiling frescoed, and in the center is suspended a six-light gilt and enamelled chandelier. . . . The golden cornices and festooned damasks indicate that Art dictated their arrangement."

Whether modest or magnificent, all the early studios shared some basic similarities. Usually they were installed on the building's top floor, with a skylight to bring daylight indoors. The subject ordinarily sat in a chair facing squarely into the camera, which was set on a tripod. To keep his head steady during exposure, he held it against a heavy wrought-iron stand with a headrest complete with clamp at the top. An adjustable mirror filled in the shadowed side of his face. Behind him was a plain cloth backdrop.

In the late 1850s the discovery of the more sensitive wet-plate, positive-negative system of photography simplified the lighting problem, but not studio décor. The simple tan or gray backdrops of earlier decades gave way to lavish painted canvases, depicting lush gardens with grapevines twining over Grecian columns, or to fancy interiors with paneled walls, staircases and marble statuary. The single chair was increased to a roomful of plush ottomans flanked by tables and balustrades, against which the subject would posture imperiously or loll seductively, depending on mood and sex.

Until well into the 20th Century, studio photography continued to mean portrait photography. But in the 1920s, the character of professional studios began to change. The increasing use of photographs in advertising meant that studios began to cater to the needs of industrial firms and fashion houses. Portrait studios remained, of course, making everything from passport photos to wedding pictures. But most of the big new studios adapted their operation to the needs of commercial clients. Some concentrated on fashion or furniture or food, some on photographing automobiles or heavy machinery. And so the major studios remain today—specialized, technically sophisticated purveyors of images to commerce and industry.

A 19th Century Portrait Parlor

◄ *A 19th Century elegance characterizes a semi-restoration of Peter Britt's Photo Gallery in Jacksonville, Oregon, with its painted canvas backdrops, two posing chairs and various props, including a flight of steps, a stuffed egret and an urn on a curved pedestal. Behind the view camera on its tripod are two wrought-iron headrests.*

Boxlike wooden view cameras (above left) were brought to Oregon from supply houses in San Francisco. One lens, with its heavy brass casing, weighed 30 pounds. Besides being a photographer, Britt was a skilled portrait painter, and examples of his art, with works by others, share the walls with his photographs. In the picture at right, above, a posing chair has been arranged against a backdrop to suggest palatial grandeur. The hole in the chair was needed for photographing babies. The mother would kneel out of sight behind the chair and hold the baby through the hole.

In Victorian America, every town worth its name boasted a photography studio. The local photographer was both resident portraitist and chronicler of town life. Every self-respecting citizen would sit importantly for his picture. Brides would pose in their wedding dresses, and young married couples would bring their first baby. On request, the photographer would lug his view camera outside for a shot on location. He would pose the fire department beside its hook and ladder, the dry-goods merchant next to his calicoes and denims, and a family in front of its new house.

The photographer of Jacksonville, Oregon, Peter Britt, arrived in town in 1852, one year after a gold strike had sent the town booming. Trained as both a portrait painter and a photographer, he set up shop with a single box camera in a log cabin he built himself. Soon people from all over southern Oregon were flocking to his studio—miners celebrating a strike, bankers in top hats, Indians, soldiers, and settlers with their families. Britt expanded to new quarters, equipped with the elegant props shown here, which are now preserved in the Jacksonville Museum.

Tintypes on Short Order

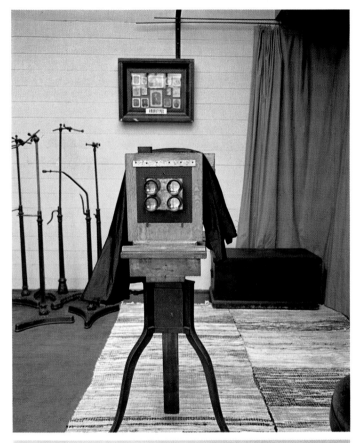

As photographic portrait galleries grew ever more lavish—and more expensive—a new kind of studio emerged that catered to the taste and pocketbook of the workingman. It was devoted exclusively to producing portraits on tintype, a fast, cheap cousin of the daguerreotype, in which the photograph was made directly on a dark metal plate that had been coated with a light-sensitive emulsion. Because of the dark metallic background, the developed picture gave the illusion of being a positive rather than a negative. Like modern Polaroids, tintypes could be taken, developed and handed over to the customer in a matter of minutes.

Tintype studios persisted until well into the 1930s, before succumbing to the more sophisticated camera techniques of modern times. But at least one still exists. At the Henry Ford Museum in Greenfield Village, a town reconstructed from America's past in Dearborn, Michigan, the tintype studio shown here has been set up in a small frame house. The visitor may still pose in front of the tintype camera like his grandfather before him, and have his image recorded for posterity on tin.

Tintype studios, like this reconstruction at Greenfield Village, were simple and functional. A monochrome background drapery hangs behind the posing chairs, an abbreviated armchair stands in the center, and a stool with a headrest is at right. The camera with its viewing cloth rests on a tripod in the center, and extra iron headrests are clustered along the left wall. A glass roof and floor-to-ceiling window admit daylight.

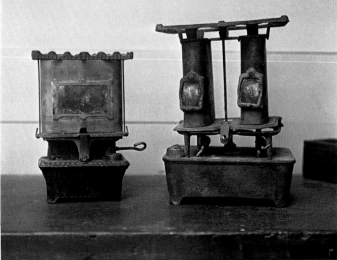

Tintype cameras, like the one at left, above, often had multiple lenses for taking several pictures at once. Since tintypes could not be printed, the only way to get a copy of a picture was to make another exposure. After the tintypes were snapped, they were developed and hung out to dry on stands like the ones at left. The entire process, from plate preparation and exposure to final portrait, took only five to ten minutes.

Splendor in the Big City

T. C. MARCEAU: *Portrait of a Lady,* date unknown

One of the most sumptuous of all the late-Victorian portrait studios was a gallery opened in New York City at the turn of the century. The studio's proprietor was a retired army officer, Colonel Theodore C. Marceau, who had already established a string of fashionable photo studios in Cincinnati, Los Angeles and San Francisco. In moving to the nation's largest city, Marceau resolved to outdo himself, and his competitors, in stylish extravagance. Although most of the city's portrait galleries were located in low-rent lofts along Broadway, Marceau splurged on a ground-floor storefront on Fifth Avenue. He then spent on furnishings and equipment what a photography journal of the day called "an amount unheard of in the establishment of photo studios." There were reception chambers and waiting rooms, and a special dressing room with an ornate marble make-up table where ladies could change into their best lace and damask evening gowns before posing decorously *(left)* in front of the camera. A fad for Middle Eastern art was currently sweeping New York society, and Marceau embellished his waiting room with Turkish draperies, carpets and ottomans.

Competing photographers scoffed at Marceau's presumption and prophesied his speedy bankruptcy. Marceau, however, not only survived, but captured a large part of the carriage trade. The bulk of his business resulted from a practice followed by fashionable ladies: they gave away framed pictures of themselves as Christmas presents. The number of sittings might rise to as many as 50 a day between Thanksgiving and Christmas. The customer would be ushered first to a dressing room to arrange her gown and hair, and then to a studio roughly 25 feet square and workmanlike in appearance, with camera, skylight or flood lamps, and the usual posing chairs and painted background panels. The photographer would take four or five different poses, and the customer would return a day or so later to choose the one she liked best. Marceau's prices were high—as much as $20 for one sitting and a dozen 5 x 7 sepia prints. But to a style-conscious society, nothing would do but a portrait from the city's fanciest gallery.

The street entrance to Colonel T. C. Marceau's ▶ posh Fifth Avenue photo gallery, with its window display of portraits in gold frames (top left), only hinted at the opulence inside. In addition to the ground-floor office and showroom (top right), there were a luxurious ladies' dressing room (bottom left), a waiting room done up to resemble a Turkish harem (bottom right) and several stories of light studios, workshops and darkrooms.

Tricks of the Trade from Hollywood

Simple or lavish, the Victorian studios never moved beyond the production of stylized portraits. But in the early 1900s a new national obsession—motion pictures—began to work dramatic changes in both the subject matter and the techniques of studio photography.

The movies seemed at first an unlikely source of photographic expertise. The earliest ones were murky one-reel shorts that flickered uneasily for five or ten minutes before expiring. They were shot in flat natural light, usually in jerry-built, open-air studios. But as directors grew more skilled, they began dressing up their product with lighting techniques, set designs and stage effects borrowed from the Broadway theater. Eventually these innovations, perfected on movie lots in Hollywood and on the East Coast, became part of the standard vocabulary of studios everywhere.

Increased realism in set design was the movies' first big contribution to studio techniques. The Jesse Lasky Feature Play Company, which from 1913 to 1915 made film adaptations of Broadway hits (above), used sets as detailed and convincing as any found behind a theater's proscenium. Innovations in lighting had to wait until the development of flood lamps. Lasky usually filmed in bright sunshine, building his sets out of doors on his Hollywood lot. Even when movie companies went inside, they splurged on huge greenhouses with glass roofs to let in the sun—like the Lubin Studio in Philadelphia (opposite), which was apparently light enough and large enough to stage three different scenes at once.

Learning to use the flood lamp was the movies' single most important breakthrough in studio techniques. It freed photographers from the flat, monotonous illumination that usually results from relying exclusively on daylight and opened up endless possibilities for creating dramatic effects.

Hollywood studios were surprisingly slow in converting to artificial light. Though the inventive Billy Bitzer, cameraman for the famous director D. W. Griffith, had used electric lighting as early as 1899—rigging some 400 arc lamps to film the Jeffries-Sharkey boxing match in New York City—Hollywood stayed with natural light until well after 1910. The main reason was economic. Sunshine was free, and in the halcyon climate of Southern California it hardly ever stopped for bad weather. But in 1915, Cecil B. De Mille began trying to duplicate the dramatic lighting effects he had learned while working at the Belasco Theater on Broadway.

De Mille first used velvet draperies and metallic reflectors to shade and direct the sunlight, but quickly switched to arc flood lamps. The results were moody and dramatic, and some scenes were so dim that De Mille's producer, Samuel Goldwyn, complained that "you couldn't see the actors' faces half the time." De Mille retorted by calling his new technique "Rembrandt lighting," which inspired Goldwyn to jack up the price of his films to movie houses. But the new lighting techniques did indeed provide an artistic and emotional impact that would have been impossible with natural light. They also gave cameramen the kind of control over their subject—even in uniformly illuminated scenes such as the one opposite—that has been an indispensable part of studio photography ever since.

Batteries of carbon-arc floodlights, some hung overhead, others mounted on standards at the sides—illuminate this early movie studio's vision of pandemonium on the New York Stock Exchange. Both for long shots and for dramatically lighted close-ups, artificial light allowed a versatility unmatched by older methods.

Pictures for the Sunday Millions

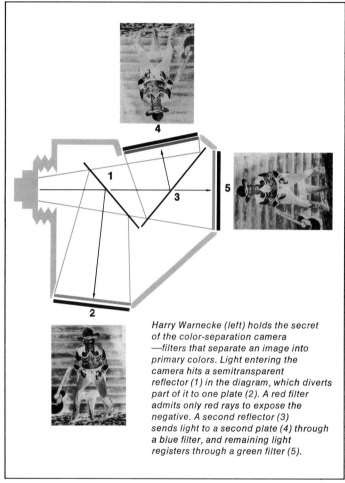

Harry Warnecke (left) holds the secret of the color-separation camera —filters that separate an image into primary colors. Light entering the camera hits a semitransparent reflector (1) in the diagram, which diverts part of it to one plate (2). A red filter admits only red rays to expose the negative. A second reflector (3) sends light to a second plate (4) through a blue filter, and remaining light registers through a green filter (5).

One of the first studios set up specifically for color photography was, paradoxically, established by a newspaper at a time when modern color film was still to be invented and ordinary newspaper letterpresses did not reproduce color photos satisfactorily. The driving force behind the idea was Harry Warnecke *(above)* a staff photographer for the New York *Daily News,* who had been experimenting with color on his

own. He knew that color could be reproduced with the rotogravure printing process, which the *News* was already using to put out a Sunday picture section that included color advertisements. He convinced his bosses that a cover photograph in full color would be a worthwhile attraction.

The *News* backed Warnecke generously. He even designed a camera of his own—a big "one-shot" device

(diagramed above) that simultaneously exposed three plates with black-and-white emulsion through three separate filters to make red, blue and green separations required for color reproduction. Using this and other specialized gear, Warnecke provided a steady supply of color pictures. And long before color snapshots were common, bathing beauties and movie stars *(opposite)* appeared in color in the *Sunday News.*

Hundreds of celebrities had their pictures snapped by Harry Warnecke's color-separation camera in the New York Daily News color studio (left), where the photographer himself adjusts the cranelike tripod that holds his bulky camera. The log cabin backdrop at the rear lent verisimilitude to the portrait of cowboy star Roy Rogers, taken in 1943. Photographers at the News studio built their own sets and created their own special effects, including a "snowstorm" of untoasted corn flakes sprinkled from a hand-cranked drum.

Fine Points of Food Photography

With new advances in lighting techniques, color and set design, studio photography had, by the 1950s, arrived at a versatility unimaginable to the early portraitists. Drawing from an increasingly sophisticated bag of photographic tricks, studio photographers gained the ability to conjure up a seemingly endless variety of special effects. They also acquired an entirely new breed of client—big business. Most large studios today work for large corporations, creating illustrations for magazine and book publishers and turning out photos for advertising agencies. This in turn has resulted in a new kind of specialization to meet the needs of commercial clients.

One of today's most important studio specialties is food photography. More money is spent advertising foods and beverages than any other kind of product—more than $2 billion per year in the late 1960s. Food photography is thus the main business of many studios, which must have special kitchen facilities in order to handle it. One such studio, shown here and on the following pages, was established in 1963 by Rudy Muller on the ground floor of a converted printing plant in New York City. In addition to a generously appointed kitchen *(above),* it contains a carpentry shop for building sets and a shooting area of some 2,300 square feet. Like most studios it is amply equipped to take pictures of nonspecialized subjects. But a full 40 per cent of its billings come from photographing food.

◀ In Rudy Muller's studio kitchen, a chef prepares a casserole of Flemish chicken that will be photographed as part of an assignment for American Home magazine. The magazine's food editor, Frances Crawford, busies herself over loaves of braided French bread. The chef, Jacques Jaffry, is employed by the client. Although Muller supplies the kitchen, the client does the cooking.

Using an 8 x 10 view camera, Rudy Muller photographs, for American Home, a still life of assorted culinary delights, including the casserole being prepared on the opposite page. To give the picture a hearty, rustic look, the dishes are arranged on a plank table and an old barn door serves as one of the two background flats. The picture will be backlit. The light source is a large boxlike strobe unit at the rear, which is aimed through the space between the two flats. Cardboard reflectors in front of the table and above the camera fill in foreground shadows, and the two bulky floor batteries attached to cables at the right provide power for the strobe.

"Planning a still photograph is like putting together a movie," says Rudy Muller. "You have to put up a set, assemble the right props, and if you're using live models you have to find a cast." No casting was needed for the *American Home* assignment, which was simply to illustrate three traditional country recipes from Europe that would provide hot, one-dish meals for winter. Nonetheless, it took two days to set up the picture and photograph it.

The first step was a conference with the magazine's food editor and art director to plan the approach and decide on a set and props. Muller then built the set with the help of two assistants, while his stylist rummaged among the city's antique and gourmet-ware shops for appropriate plates, casserole dishes, pitchers and glassware. The next morning, a chef arrived from *American Home* to cook the food, which included a French *cassoulet* of beans and meat, Flemish-style chicken with cream and vegetables, and a stuffed cabbage. To make sure that the food would look fresh and appetizing during the entire shooting session, each dish was prepared in duplicate; when the first set of dishes became cold, it was replaced with the second set, which had been kept warm in the oven. As soon as the food was ready, it was arranged attractively on a table, the lighting was adjusted, and the shooting began. Muller photographed steadily for two hours, using both a 35mm reflex and an 8 x 10 view camera, and finally produced the picture on the opposite page.

Before shooting, Muller rearranges pieces of Flemish-style chicken in an earthenware casserole (above left) to make them more photogenic. He then photographs the assembled dishes with a 35mm camera (center), searching for unusual angles and depth-of-field effects. To create the effect of steam rising from the casseroles, an assistant gets ready to pump a liquefied titanium compound into the air above them. The chemical reacts with the air to produce a billowy, steamlike vapor.

RUDY MULLER: *One-Dish Meals*, 1970

*The photograph picked to run in the magazine
gives a hearty, down-home look to this array of
sturdy provincial dishes, each one a meal in
itself. The cassoulet is in the casserole at left,
the chicken in the earthenware baking dish in
the center, and the stuffed cabbage with tomato
sauce on the plate at right. The rustic wine
carafe, butter pot and lusterware pitcher were
chosen to enhance the country-kitchen effect.*

Producing Settings on Demand

One particularly specialized kind of studio photography is taking pictures of room settings. Furniture and fabric manufacturers, carpetmakers and makers of lighting fixtures all like to display their wares as though they had already been purchased and comfortably installed in the buyer's home. So for advertising photos they generally turn to studios that concentrate on designing and building homelike environments that attempt to give a lived-with look to a contemporary dining-room suite or an ensemble of matched bed sheets and window curtains.

A leading specialist in room-setting photography is Lionel Freedman, who in 1947 established his studio in New York City in a converted theater. There is something theatrical, in fact, about the whole Freedman establishment. He stages a photograph as though he were producing a play. The set is planned with the client in a conference room located on what was once the theater's balcony. It is designed by Freedman himself, who holds a degree in architecture from New York University. Sets are constructed and painted in a carpentry shop in the old backstage area and nailed together in the orchestra, where the photograph is shot. The final picture, processed in a darkroom in the balcony, is billed at orchestra prices —a minimum rate of $1,500 for a single-page advertisement designed to appear in a national magazine.

Working at a drafting table in his office (above left), Lionel Freedman designs a room setting for a client. The set will be built on the studio floor (left), and photographed with the view camera that is shown. The lighting console in the foreground works in much the same way as a stage electrician's light panel to produce an almost infinite variety of special effects.

In the orchestra of the converted theater that serves as Freedman's studio, an assistant assembles a room setting from a stockpile of flats and props. Freedman meanwhile roughs out another sketch in his office off the left side of the balcony. Freedman employs two assistants and occasionally hires professional carpenters and freelance stylists to help on difficult jobs.

This scaffoldlike object assembled from wooden
struts in Lionel Freedman's studio is a 12-sided
dome. It will provide the framework for a room
setting designed to complement an arrangement
of modern chairs, tables and bookcases. The
client, S & H Green Stamps, will use the resulting
photograph in a catalogue to show the various
items—including furniture—that can be obtained
for appropriate numbers of trading stamps.

LIONEL FREEDMAN: *Beach House*, 1970

The setting for the final photograph is a beach
house filled with S & H furnishings. There are
clean-lined tables, a chromium stand, a sectional
bookcase and, hanging from a strut, an Op
Art reproduction. The two models ease back into
chairs: the man in one built like an enormous
plastic-covered bean bag, the woman in a
recliner. Two rear-projection screens provide the
exterior background of beach and ocean.

Snow Scenes in July

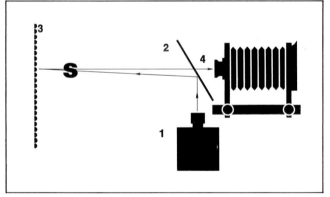

Versatility is the special strength of Pohlman Studios in Milwaukee, whose clients are mostly large manufacturing companies. Its facilities are so extensive that it can make almost any kind of photograph of any marketable product, from ketchup bottles to sailing yachts. One device allows products to be photographed in any imaginable setting without leaving the studio. Called a front projection system, it creates the same kind of panoramic vistas that early photographers produced with painted backdrops—but with far greater realism. Its components are a slide projector, a large screen with a special reflecting surface and a lightly silvered, see-through mirror that deflects light rays coming from one direction, but lets through rays coming from other directions *(diagram, right)*. By projecting the appropriate transparency, the photographer can shoot a sports car on a Daytona track, a surfer on a Hawaiian beach or a snowmobile *(opposite)*—all in Milwaukee in the middle of July.

Pohlman's front projection system creates the setting for a snowmobile ad. In the picture at left above, the photographer sets up his shot. The top picture shows the photographer by his camera, visible through the hooded mirror. The slide projector is below the camera lens, and the snowmobile is reflected in the mirror set behind the photographer's hand. The diagram illustrates the projection rig. The slide projector (1) beams a snow scene up at the lightly silvered see-through mirror (2), angled at exactly 45° in front of the camera. The mirror directs the image to the big screen (3). The snowmobile stands in front of the screen at S. The screen's surface has the ability to reflect light directly back toward its source, concentrating it so that the background seems very brightly lit. The intensified image returns through the mirror to the lens of the camera (4).

POHLMAN STUDIOS: *Snowmobile*, 1970

*Though shot in the studio, the snowmobile and
models seem to be outside on location. By
carefully adjusting the lighting on the subject to
match the brightness of the snowscape projected
onto the background screen, the photographer
has made the two blend together. The only props
were plastic snow and the pine tree at right.*

Room for Rent

The most unusual of all contemporary studios contains no cameras or darkrooms, not a single flood lamp or strobe unit. No photographers' names appear on its letterhead. Yet it provides two invaluable facilities for photographers —plentiful space and superb sets.

Classic Displays Incorporated started business in 1947 in New York City as an all-purpose set-design company. It planned and built displays for exhibition booths at trade fairs, showrooms for furniture stores, sets for fashion shows and window displays for department stores. But its talent for putting together distinguished sets on short notice quickly attracted photographers, who often need sets in a hurry but have neither space to house them nor facilities for constructing them. A photographer could order a set in the afternoon, and by next morning one would be built and ready for shooting.

As photography became an ever-greater part of CDI's business, and took over more and more of its floor space, CDI's founder Fred Rathe expanded into ampler quarters. In 1956 he purchased an entire six-story Victorian brick building *(opposite)* in New York City's Chelsea district. Like many other New York studios, the building is something of a mongrel. Built in 1903 as a stable for the draft horses that once

pulled streetcars for the Fifth Avenue Coach Company, it has also been used as the headquarters of the Broadway stage-design firm of Nolan Brothers. Rathe converted it, installing carpentry shops, a metalworking shop, conference rooms, dressing rooms for models, and two studios measuring some 50 by 80 feet, which are rented out to photographers by the day. Because of its large size, and the multi-ton carrying capacity of its freight elevator, CDI is one of the few studios in the city equipped to handle large machinery, such as automobiles and trucks. Richard Avedon once used it to photograph an elephant, painted pink.

CDI is still a jack-of-all-trades in set design. "We build any kind of anything, for anybody," boasts the production manager Martin Freedgood. In addition to the usual trade exhibits and fashion shows, CDI has staged spectaculars such as the Hong Kong pavilion at the 1964-1965 New York World's Fair, for which it built three Chinese junks, the largest 40 feet long with a 32-foot mast. But photography seems to inspire its greatest feats of scenic legerdemain. It has churned up a rainstorm, built a miniature replica of Moscow's Red Square, and even created an Arctic ice floe, with styrofoam icebergs floating in a 60-foot-long ocean of real water. □

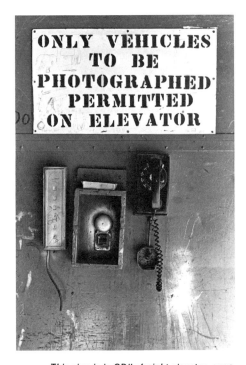

This sign is in CDI's freight elevator, once used to transport horses. Now it lifts automobiles up to the main studio area on the top floor of the fortresslike structure opposite, which was originally built as a horse barn.

Carpentry shops cover one entire floor of the CDI studio and spill over onto part of another. Here employees knock together flats, paint sets, prefabricate display booths and room settings for photographers and other commercial clients. The carpenters sometimes put in 80-hour weeks, working day and night to complete rush assignments. The workman in the picture on the opposite page, top left, puts finishing touches on a segment of a wooden archway for a trade fair; completed segments rest on his worktable. Another workman (opposite, bottom left) uses a band saw to cut a filigree in a board. To save time, sets are often fastened together with heavy-duty staple guns (opposite, top right) rather than hammer and nails. But more permanent props, such as the bookcase at bottom right, opposite, demand a cabinetmaker's painstaking skills.

In the main studio area on the top floor of the CDI
building, a workman paints the cyclorama, a 70-
foot-long plaster arc used as a permanent
backdrop for photographs. The studio covers
some 3,000 square feet and is 20 feet high. A tower
above the roof allows camera heights of 30 feet.

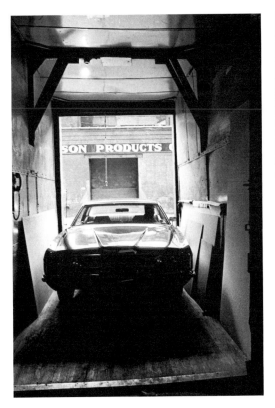

CDI's heavy-duty freight elevator (above left) lifts a Ford Galaxie to the top-floor studio to be photographed for an ad. In the studio (above), a photographer lines up a shot of another car already parked in the cyclorama. Baffles at the right of the cyclorama and a ceiling of seamless paper direct light toward the subject. Since the sides of the cyclorama are curved, and the base slopes forward to meet the floor, avoiding a square joint, objects photographed within it appear to be suspended in infinite space.

A rain studio in CDI's ground-floor garage provides showers or hurricanes on order. The rain machine is simplicity itself—an overhead, perforated tin basin attached to a hose. Yet with appropriate backdrops, fans for simulating wind, and light reflectors (the umbrella at right in the picture above is for filling in shadows, not for keeping dry), photographers can blow up a thoroughly convincing rainstorm for overshoe and raincoat ads such as the shot at left.

The Studio on Location 3

Members of the studio team at the major New ▶
York firm of Horn/Griner gather on an office
stairway for a group portrait. At rear, under the
"G" of the firm's logotype, is general manager
Hal Siegman, wearing glasses and mustache.
Around him are people holding a variety of jobs,
from photographer's assistant and bookkeeper to
members of the television production unit.

The Photographer's Team

The look is rich hippie, the atmosphere is casual, the pace is very New York at the Horn/Griner photographic studio on East 54th Street. The studios and dressing rooms are on the first floors of adjacent two-story buildings. Downstairs, in the basement offices, the general manager, Hal Siegman, refuses to become flustered although six telephones are ringing at once and half a dozen assistants keep stopping by his desk for advice or instructions. Siegman is a former newspaperman and has learned to be the calm eye of the storm.

Upstairs Steve Horn is shooting a fashion picture in the studio, a huge bare room that looks like a parking garage spookily empty of cars. In one corner a set has been put up. It is a vine-covered porch of a beach house, decorated with white wicker furniture. Three models come out of the adjoining dressing room, attired in beachwear. Horn, tall and thin, with longish blond hair and a mauve T-shirt sporting an appliquéd butterfly, gives instructions to the girls. They drape themselves over the porch railing. Steve suggests that one of them (his wife, incidentally) strike a pose beside a wicker table. An assistant takes a reading with a light meter, while another man snaps a Polaroid test shot.

The art director and the copywriter from the advertising agency are wandering about, talking to a woman who represents the beachwear manufacturer. She points out that one of the costumes is a bit wrinkled. The message is passed along, and the skirt is handed to a wardrobe mistress who is standing beside an ironing board, prepared for just such an emergency. (Meanwhile a robe has been handed to the model.) A hairdresser follows a model around, combing out an uncooperative curl. A stylist, or prop girl, fusses with the arrangement of china on the wicker table. Horn says he thinks the blue-and-white pattern on the teapot is distractingly large and she replaces it with something in a smaller pattern. An animal trainer arrives with a squirrel in a cage. "No, forget the squirrel, I've decided against it," the art director says. The animal trainer goes away.

Horn asks for some music and gets it: hard rock blaring from a record player. A strobe light goes dead and an assistant speedily replaces it. A hanging plant keeps tangling in the hair of one of the models; the stylist snips off the vine. The art director has drawn a sketch to convey a notion of how the photograph should look; Horn consults the drawing and then steps up on a box to check the angle of his shot. He asks the models to assume a languid pose, an "unposed" look. The girls droop and appear to relax. "Terrific, that's perfect," he murmurs. "Can you move your leg a bit to the left, Vicki?" The stylist rearranges a fold on a beach robe. Horn fiddles with his camera, already loaded by an assistant; the hairdresser bounds back on the set for a final tug at a floating wisp; the shooting begins. Horn talks lovingly to the models, urges them to relax, suggests a new pose, brings them together by the porch rail, then sends one off to one side. He asks one girl to sit. She sits down and rests her feet on another chair. The music gets louder and faster.

There are dozens of commercial studios that operate like Horn/Griner, doing a general business, including television commercials, although few are as large. (A few studios cranking out illustrations for mail-order catalogues are probably the largest of all.) They are all engaged in complex assignments that require close cooperation among the many specialists who make up the studio team. Running a studio is like flying a plane, as the versatile studio photographer Irving Penn once remarked. Both jobs involve very expensive, delicate pieces of 20th Century equipment. If the photographer is the captain of the plane, he must nevertheless rely on his crew to carry out his orders and anticipate his wishes.

The number of people on the team can vary greatly. The Horn/Griner studio is unusual in that more than 25 people work there full time. A representative goes out among advertising agencies and drums up business. He shows samples of his clients' work, discusses fees and scheduling, and if he makes a sale, he sets up a tentative shooting date. Once the job comes into the studio Hal Siegman, as general manager, takes charge. He sits at a desk overflowing with papers, beneath a bulletin board littered with snapshots of Victorian ladies, postcards showing Renaissance paintings, joke mottoes and posters. Despite the air of arty disorder, Siegman runs a tight ship. He has huge maps of New York and its environs punctured with pushpins indicating various locations for every possible kind of interior and exterior shot. The maps are coordinated with a subject file of cards. If an assignment calls for the front of a candy store, Siegman looks under "C" and finds a choice of four. Each storefront is pictured in a Polaroid snapshot under a typed entry that gives the name of the store's owner and the charge for a day's shooting; usually it will cost about $100.

Few details of the studio are overlooked. Every key to every lock in the studio (even to the bubble gum machine) is tagged and hung on a pegboard. Props are alphabetized and filed away in closets lining one long wall. Tools, nails, screws, staples are all kept in labeled boxes and jars. "We're able to do 25 per cent more work than other studios of the same size," Siegman says proudly, "because we're so efficient."

This efficiency and resourcefulness are often tested to the limit. One difficult advertising assignment that Horn/Griner undertook a few years ago was to produce a believable replica of Noah's Ark. An art director had the idea of placing two models wearing raincoats (the product) on the ark itself, surrounded by dozens of animals—naturally in twos. There are some animals, however, that refuse to pose for a camera side by side: lions and birds, for instance. And where do you find two elephants on short notice?

Siegman assigned the building of the ark to Stanley Glaubach, a well-known display designer. After some snooping, he discovered that there were two elephants in the African Pavilion at the New York World's Fair, then being held in Queens. After many phone calls, Siegman obtained permission to photograph the elephants and to use the fairgrounds—as long as the photographers were off the grounds by the time the first customers began to arrive at 7:30 a.m. A taxidermist and the New York Museum of Natural History agreed to supply stuffed lions, zebras, deer and birds, for a fee. Animal-talent agencies promised monkeys, sheep and a bear cub. On the shooting day a caravan of vans transported ark and animals out to the fairgrounds by 5 a.m. and within an hour all of the animals, stuffed and alive, had been posed beside the human models. A stroke of luck made the early morning sky broodingly cloudy, actually threatening rain.

While Siegman cannot control the weather, he is so persuasive on the telephone that he has obtained tanks from the Army and a submarine from the Navy. In setting up a picture that was supposed to suggest a presidential press conference, he found someone who looked exactly like President Richard Nixon (from the back) and a hotel ballroom that seemed to have been copied from the East Room of the White House, where the actual conferences are held. In arranging for a public-service advertisement assailing poor housing conditions in Harlem, Siegman sent his assistants out in search of a slum apartment that was suitably ghastly as well as unoccupied and available—a hard combination to come up with, since slum landlords were understandably reluctant to have their ugly tenements photographed.

Usually there are four full-time assistants working at the Horn/Griner studio, not only performing legwork for Siegman but also setting up shots for the photographers. Much studio photography is plain housework, performed by the assistants: checking and cleaning equipment, keeping track of the gloves needed for changing filters over lights, vacuuming, washing prop dishes, changing film. Some of the assistants are aspiring young photographers; 10 to 15 come by every week for an interview with Siegman, showing him their portfolios in the hope of obtaining a job in which to learn the business from the bottom up. Siegman sees them all and keeps their names in a file. He never knows when he will need to hire someone on short notice, because few assistants work at Horn/Griner longer than six months or a year. The studio has been in business since 1954 and dozens of assistants have become well-known photographers in their own right.

When an assignment comes into the office, Siegman receives little more than a hasty pencil sketch from the art director at the advertising agency. He decodes the sketch and the scribbled descriptions of the types of models wanted and makes out a list, which he hands over to the casting director ("middle-aged Midwestern housewife, two-year-old boy, black-and-white mutt"). The casting director, Mrs. Jackie Wilder, consults the art director and gets a more precise notion of exactly what sort of housewife he wants. Should she be tall? Skinny? Must she be pretty, or should she be a "character" type? Sometimes the client must be consulted too, particularly if the model is going to be used throughout an entire advertising campaign to help establish the client's image.

Mrs. Wilder has no trouble finding models. "They're coming out of the woodwork," she says. "Yesterday the delivery boy from the deli chased me all over the office, pleading with me to use him in an ad. Everyone wants to model. Retired insurance men and certified public accountants come in off the street. If they look interesting, we take a Polaroid of them and keep it on hand." Mrs. Wilder prefers to use actors because she feels they know how to respond to photographers' suggestions and assume a role, not simply be lovely and bland. She goes to off-off-Broadway plays and cabarets in search of good actors and arresting faces. Other casting directors she knows approach strangers in restaurants, in elevators or on the street, but Mrs. Wilder can't quite bring herself to do that, nor does she need to. When she has glanced through all her Polaroids of insurance salesmen and seen dozens of models from the agencies, she narrows her list down to first, second and third choices for each role. Usually, clients go along with the first choice.

While Mrs. Wilder is casting the picture, one of the studio's stylists consults the art director's sketch and seeks out the props that will be needed. Stylists are the unsung heroines of commercial photography, for, to a large extent, the final look of any studio photograph is their doing. They give exact instructions to the set builders, usually a company that constructs vine-covered porches and Noah's Arks for photographers, and window displays for department stores and stage sets as well. The stylists also must find all the things that are seen in a picture—the teacups, the clothes, the paintings in the background and the client's television set in the foreground.

Few studios, of course, require so many full-time specialists—business manager, casting director, hairdresser, wardrobe mistress, stylist—and most rely upon freelance people, many of whom offer highly individualized skills. The most commonly used freelance specialist is the stylist, who frequently combines a number of talents. One such is Louise Effron, a chic young woman who lives in an elegant Manhattan apartment with fur throws on the bed and on the floor, and a clutch of giant ostrich eggs—which she got at a "terrific bargain." Each of her assignments, which she usually receives from a photographer but occasionally directly from an advertising agency, is utterly new, and she never has longer than a week to work on it. On one job she had to re-create Custer's Last Stand and she had only a few days to do it. She hurried to the public library, flipped through books on Custer, studied all available photographs of him and cast a near look-alike for the part. Then she hopped a westbound plane, chose a desert site on a ranch, hired make-up men and two dozen Indians reputed to be excellent bareback riders. The ranch owner supplied Custer's men, and horses for everyone. Miss Effron rented authentic costumes from a Hollywood studio for the soldiers and their famous commanding officer.

The agency art director had drawn a sketch showing Custer standing with one foot on a dead horse. Miss Effron found a handsome animal that its trainer guaranteed would play dead on command. On the shooting day, however, the horse refused to cooperate and she had to call a veterinarian, who was supposed to administer a sedative to the animal. But horses can be knocked out for only 40 seconds; any longer, and their lives are endangered. Forty seconds, unfortunately, was not long enough to coordinate all the elements in the shot (the Indians had to be circling the encampment, while the soldiers staggered about stuck with arrows and splashed with fake blood). So they gave up on the horse. When the picture was finally ready for publication, the client turned it down. An important figure in public life had just been assassinated, and the client, a soft-drink manufacturer, rightly felt that a pictorial reference to the bloody battle of the Little Big Horn might seem tasteless.

Most freelance stylists work by the day. They get large fees plus expenses, and they generally deserve every penny. They know which antique stores will rent furniture for photographs; which garment manufacturers will lend ball gowns or bikinis in return for a credit line; where one can find an empty living room in Manhattan exactly 20 by 22 feet with a bay window, a parquet floor and a chandelier; where there is a beach on Long Island that looks exactly like a Caribbean island; which baker can turn out really elegant marzipan; and how to make a cat stare into a fishbowl (you smear the bowl with food or catnip). They know that you can get a wonderfully wrinkled 90-year-old man from the Funnyface Brigade, a model agency, and that, if your budget is limited, you can hire a certain model who will look like five different girls in five different photographs. Louise Effron has a degree in art history and she is able to tell a seamstress at a costume house exactly how to remodel a dress so that it looks like something Marie Antoinette might have worn. She also knows her way around an architectural library and can sketch designs for a Georgian exterior or a Regency interior, hand them over to a display house and give precise instructions to the carpenters.

Yvonne McHarg, another freelance stylist, can also move mountains in a few seconds. Her biggest assignment came one day when a company that was running a sweepstakes decided to run an advertisement showing all of the 500 prizes in one photograph. Some of the prizes were large—a car, a trailer, an airplane, an inflatable swimming pool. The New York weather was terrible and so she figured the picture should be shot in California. In Los Angeles, she found a playground that could be rented for a few days. Then she began to assemble the prizes. The mink coat, the washing machine and the beach buggy presented no problems. But the airplane had too wide a wingspan to get through the streets on a truck; Miss McHarg found a mechanic who could take wings off and put them back on again. In three days she had managed to bring all the products together and to arrange for a 20-foot scaffold to be built, from which the photographer could get his shots of the entire playground. A child had been hired to ride the prize pony (rented from a Hollywood studio); women had been recruited to stand beside the washing machine and the steam iron; teenagers had been found to splash around with abandon in the pool.

On the night before the shooting it started to rain. Miss McHarg hired a limousine and bought yards of plastic tarpaulin from department stores and used-car lots. She hurried back and threw plastic over everything. A guard was hired to stand watch over the playground until morning. The next day the weather cleared, the picture was taken, Miss McHarg arranged for everything to be shipped back to the client—and the job was over. A few days later she was back in New York, desperately looking for moss and heather to construct an artificial Scottish moor. The heather was easy but she spent hours on the phone trying to find enough moss. Finally the manager of a Brooklyn greenhouse said that he had plenty of moss—but his men were too busy to scrape it off the floor. A big snowstorm had struck New York; streets were blocked and taxis had vanished. Equipped with a shovel and dozens of boxes, Miss McHarg took the subway to Brooklyn, scraped and dug for hours, and carted her precious moss home on the subway.

"My life is really unbelievable," she declares. "Not too long ago I had to find a deer for the Christmas cover of a magazine. I located a man who brought his deer into town in the back of his station wagon. Lovely beast. Great rack of antlers. He brought the deer up to the studio on the elevator and then told us he had double-parked, but would be back in a jiffy. No sooner was its master gone, however, than the deer broke into sobs. Well, not really sobs, but tiny mewings, like a kitten. The deer started running about very nervously, its hooves slipping on the shiny vinyl floor. I didn't know what to do. I finally just threw my arms around its head and let it cry itself out on my shoulder. Finally the poor deer calmed down and we got our picture."

Miss McHarg's specialty is food photography. She has impeccable taste and can set a table worthy of a duchess's dining room. She does everything from designing the wallpaper in the background to selecting the right salt and pepper shakers, from costuming the models to making sure the roast is rare. Like most stylists, she usually comes to every sitting with alternative choices for every prop so that the photographer, the art director and the client can take their pick of platters, tablecloths or ties for the male model.

Photographic home economists are other members of the studio team who are almost always hired on a freelance basis. Mrs. Zenja Cary works with two full-time assistants and prepares food not only for still photographs (she has cooked many a LIFE "Great Dinner") but also for commercials on television and feature films. She taught Dustin Hoffman how to make a soufflé for the movie *John and Mary,* and says he was an apt pupil. Meats are usually undercooked since under bright lights they often look darker and drier than they do when served at dinner. If a turkey is cooked until it is done, its skin begins to shrivel as it cools; fish is often broiled only on one side, because turning the fish may cause it to flake and pull apart.

Greens like celery or lettuce are a special photographic problem. Their colors are so pale that they sometimes come out white in a color photograph. Mrs. Cary knows that she must buy five heads of lettuce, even if only two leaves are needed for the picture; she must be able to select two very dark green and perfectly fresh leaves for the lens. She disapproves of faking the color of vegetables, but some food subjects, like lime sherbet, for example, must have coloring added to show the natural colors in the photograph.

Hot foods present their own problems, especially if they are supposed to be steaming when the picture is taken. Often the cook will let the photographer set up his picture with a look-alike stand-in roast or steak and then at the last minute replace it with the actual meat, hot from the oven. If the cook is less concerned with scrupulous realism, she can pour steaming gravy over a lukewarm roast just before the shutter snaps, or conceal a pan of simmering water on a hot plate behind the meat. One week Mrs. Cary prepared many soufflés in order to illustrate one for a magazine recipe. When a soufflé has risen high above its mold, it holds its shape for only half a minute before it falls. Mrs. Cary had the photographer set up his camera a few feet from her stove. When each soufflé was ready she shouted, "Come and get it!" The assistant whisked the soufflé in front of the camera, the photographer shot —and after a dozen tries they got a satisfactory picture.

Rather than assemble a full-scale ark or hire a couple of dozen Indians to gallop around a latter-day Custer, studio photographers sometimes employ freelance model-builders as members of their teams. If a textbook publisher wants a picture of the barbarians attacking Rome, a photographer can arrange for a builder of three-dimensional models to do the job.

A hairdresser is another functionary invariably laid on for fashion assignments. Photographic hair stylists' work is sometimes quite a bit more exaggerated than ordinary hair fashions, but for the most part their only "trick" is that they are very good—so good that the best make $400 a day.

Once the picture has been taken, the studio photographer sometimes must enlist the aid of color retouchers. If a photographer has built a house and laid a lawn in his studio, for instance, and assembled 16 highly paid models for the photograph, the expense of redoing the picture would be prohibitive. But upon examining the color transparency, he may notice that there are scratches on the emulsion or a dangling strobe-light wire shows in one corner or a blemish stands out on one model's face. Or the art director from the advertising agency may decide that he wants another inch of grass at the bottom of the picture so that he can run printed words across it. Instead of starting all over again, the photographer will ask the color-retouching house to paint over the scratches, wires or blemishes or paint in another inch of grass. The color retouchers are super-realist painters. They generally work on the original transparency and paint directly on it with delicate brushes and dyes, first blocking out portions that do not need to be retouched with masks of adhesive acetate. If the work is very complex, or the film 2¼ inch or smaller, they will make an 8 x 10 duplicate first. Retouchers are also indispensable when an assignment calls for a trick shot—an airplane perching on an offshore oil rig, for instance. The color retouchers can make composites of such a scene either by fitting the two elements and fusing them together with acetone, or by exposing the desired portion of each picture in multiple sequence on a new transparency.

Studio photography, whether used to illustrate cookbooks or advertisements for soft drinks, art magazines or history texts, always depends on the teamwork of these stylists, hairdressers, wardrobe mistresses, home economists or model-builders. But no matter how clever or efficient a team member may be, his worth ultimately depends on his ability to understand the photographer's needs and to second-guess his problems. A studio like Horn/Griner operates on a working budget of more than $10,000 a week; Steve Horn and Norman Griner have to take pictures on a very tight schedule to meet their payroll. Unless they are efficiently supported by their team, unless their minds are freed to concentrate on strictly photographic problems, their work will suffer. For that reason every member of the team must be both a mind reader and a bit of a photographer himself. The casting director must know what sort of model will respond to a particular photographer's ideas and muttered directions. The stylist must know that the photographer loathes blue teapots and overstuffed chairs—and she must design a set that will photograph well from several different angles. Every assistant must know when to tell the photographer that a light needs adjustment and when to keep his mouth shut. Because, in the end, unless the photographer brings off the perfect picture, all his helpers' help has gone to waste. ☐

On the Subject's Home Grounds

The test of the studio photographer comes when he discovers that the picture he wants to make cannot be shot on his home grounds—when, despite the existence of stylists, props, models and all the equipment to which a man can readily lay a hand, he must go on a pilgrimage, taking studio to subject. There, on location, he must achieve the technical perfection of studio work.

At times, the reasons for taking the studio on location are obvious. Heads of state seldom can find the time to visit a photographer's studio: to take the picture opposite, Arnold Newman, who is based in New York, had to set up the essentials of a studio in the Oval Room office of the President in Washington. At other times, the reasons for going on location with the studio are more subtle. It is possible—if complicated—to create in the studio a snowy woodland scene for a surprisingly realistic pic-

ture of winter sports equipment *(pages 68-69).* But there are many abstract ideas that are difficult to capture except on location. To best express the drama of two thousand years of Christianity, Newman went to Jerusalem and set up a studio in a street at dawn. Many another studio photographer has made a one-hour trip from Manhattan to Brooklyn—or spent months traveling across the world—in search of atmospheric locales essential to his pictures.

Whether he travels with elaborate setups, taking along a specially designed tent as does Irving Penn *(pages 98-99)* or a minimum of gear as did Louise Dahl-Wolfe *(pages 92-93),* the studio photographer on location carries with him one vital, indiscernible piece of control equipment: his own mind. Therein, as Newman says, lies his purpose—to "get, or try to get, the kind of a picture you imagined before you left."

When Arnold Newman was asked to make a ▶ portrait of President Lyndon B. Johnson in 1963, he took his studio equipment to the Oval Room in the White House. Newman was given 90 minutes to arrange his equipment, but only 15 minutes for the actual shooting. The photographer covered the windows with cloths to block unwanted light, mounted two view cameras—a 4 x 5 and an 8 x 10 —and arranged his lights and reflectors, using an assistant as a stand-in. While making his picture (opposite), Newman coaxed the President into the poses and facial expressions he wanted, as a Secret Service man watched in the background.

Shortly after the Six-Day War of 1967 between Arab and Israeli forces, in which Jerusalem fell to Israel, *Holiday* assigned Arnold Newman to make photographs symbolizing the three great religions—Christianity, Judaism and Islam—whose histories are bound to the Holy City. Newman and his editor realized that such pictures could be taken only on location, in Jerusalem.

Before setting out, Newman blocked out each photograph in his mind, and selected the props he would need. Once in Jerusalem he decided to shoot the Christianity picture on the Via Dolorosa, the narrow street along which tradition says Christ carried the Cross on His way to the Crucifixion. The site is that of the Fifth Station of the Cross, where Simon of Cyrene stepped forward to help Jesus carry the Cross. For the picture *(opposite),* the King James Bible was opened to Matthew 27:32, where the story of Simon is told.

Crowded into a narrow ancient street—and guarded against Arab snipers by Israeli soldiers —Newman set up religious articles before his view camera for the picture opposite. Since it was shot at dawn, the natural light was bolstered by floodlights and spotlights with reflectors.

Summing up the spirit of Christianity, a plain ▶ Cross borrowed from a nearby church rests against a wall of the Via Dolorosa. The pennon with the Cross on its flagstaff's tip and the weapons represent the Christian Crusaders who fought to drive the Moslems from Jerusalem.

ARNOLD NEWMAN: *Christianity, the Fifth Station of the Cross*, 1967

Working out of a Suitcase

When the noted fashion photographer Louise Dahl-Wolfe undertook a quest for unusual locales in the years after World War II, the better to display high-style clothes, she resolved to remain a studio photographer but to travel light —without boxes of props or elaborate equipment. She had to rely upon her own ability to exploit natural lighting and upon finding props on the spot to produce studio-quality pictures. She succeeded brilliantly, returning from exotic places with exquisite pictures. By artfully incorporating local architecture and handiwork *(opposite)* into her photographs, Mrs. Dahl-Wolfe demonstrated that the studio is defined by the photographer's mind—which keeps control of the subject matter whether in Marrakech or on Madison Avenue.

Ready to depart an estate in Hammamet, Tunisia, where she shot fashion pictures for Harper's Bazaar, Louise Dahl-Wolfe (above, far right) used a self-timer to trip the shutter for this picture of her troupe and herself. Her model, Natalie, stands at the group's left—and the car roof bears cases containing dresses and her view camera.

In the shade of a Tunisian tree, Natalie wears ▶ *cuffed shorts and blouse of rayon faille—an image of cool sophistication created by careful use of natural light. The exotic props—two pairs of love birds in filigreed cages—were obtained locally.*

LOUISE DAHL-WOLFE: *Sportswear in Tunisia*, 1950

Instant Setting in an Empty Flat

Rudy Muller is a New York photographer and former antique dealer noted for his appropriate choices of props. He often wins commissions because his imaginative studio sets give an added dimension of realism to the message an advertiser wishes to convey. If an outdoor setting or a tight schedule makes building a set impractical, Muller finds a scene to match his idea and simply takes the studio on location.

For a 24-page newspaper advertising supplement planned by a wine and liquor importer, Muller conceived nine different parties at which the products might be used. To establish a mood of youthful gaiety for a "moving-in" party *(overleaf),* he chose an empty flat in Brooklyn's Park Slope district. Old town houses there were drawing an influx of New Yorkers who liked the high ceilings, bay windows and cavernous rooms—attractions that Muller saw as well suited to his own purposes. He rented the flat for a day, made it a studio, set the scene, shot the pictures and was out by nightfall.

Forethought is the key to this kind of operation; once on location the photographer must be self-sufficient. Muller's studio equipment—cameras, lights, extension cords, stands, tool kit and ladders—filled a station wagon. A second station wagon, timed to arrive an hour later, carried the props for the party scene—food, tableware, barrels, packing crates and the client's wines.

One of Muller's assistants (nearer the camera) lends a hand to a moving man in the photographer's Manhattan studio as they prepare to pack for the trip to Brooklyn. Everything needed to set up a studio-on-location had been previously assembled; careful tallies of equipment were made at both ends of the journey.

A stepladder and big cardboard reflectors are
among the first items to be lugged up to the
apartment chosen for location shooting. Muller's
crew transformed the bare living room into a
studio, swept and dusted, and staged the scene he
imagined for a young couple's moving-in party.

Muller (in doorway, rear) approves the hostess gown the model will wear at the moving-in party he is staging in the empty apartment. The models had arrived on location right on schedule, about two and a half hours after the first load of equipment came. By that time the studio was essentially set up: lights, reflectors and cameras had been placed by Muller's assistant; the party scene was ready for the last touches.

With her dress carefully hung up, Muller's "hostess" crouches in front of a mirror previous tenants had left in the apartment bathroom, perfecting her make-up for the final shot.

Muller hand-held his Nikon F for the final photograph at right. The couple are almost ready for their guests. The dinner—onion soup, roast smoked pork loin, hot French bread, fruit and cheeses, which the "host" is unpacking—will be served with champagne and Italian wines. Muller artfully placed a fruit basket on the mantel to hide an ugly light fixture. The antique tureen, crystal stemware, Revere bowl and pistol-grip carvers imply the comfortable background of a lighthearted young couple who offer barrels and crates as tables and seats at their moving-in party—but have the taste to serve the advertiser's wines.

RUDY MULLER: *We-Just-Moved-In Party*, 1970

Irving Penn's Neutral Ground

In making a long series of documentary portrait essays that have taken him to remote parts of the world, Irving Penn has chosen to work in what he calls "neutral ground," where the subject, removed from his natural surroundings, lowers his guard and presents a true aspect of himself to the photographer and camera. This means using a studio. Penn discovered the value of such neutral ground in 1945 during a Christmas visit to Cuzco, Peru. There he rented a local photographer's portrait studio where, in three days, he made a number of photographs that Edward Steichen said "richly render the timelessness and human dignity of a people." *Vogue* later assigned Penn to carry out a series of location-shot studio studies of little-known cultures.

For most of these assignments Penn hired studios. In Spain and Crete he improvised, using bare walls of farmhouses and garages as backgrounds and employing the Mediterranean light as he would floods and spots. But in 1967 when his search for authentic locations and unspoiled peoples led him to the indigenous cultures of Dahomey on Af-

rica's West Coast *(overleaf),* he knew he could not count even on improvised studios; he would have to take one with him. He devised a portable studio that he "could bring to the subject, rather than vice versa." This ultimate studio-on-location *(opposite)* has accompanied Penn on all his later documentary expeditions, allowing him the desired control of conditions for his pictures.

Penn also brings personal assets to the job of photographing exotic peoples. A man of natural reserve and formality, he is nonetheless able to break through language and cultural barriers to elicit an equally serious response from his sitters, who become his rapt partners, rather than uninvolved subjects of snapshots.

As Penn describes his aim: "I have tried to find universal and timeless qualities . . . rather than to record accidental or transitory situations. At the same time, I also am always sustained by awareness of the documentary and historical value of these records . . . because tomorrow or next year much of what I photographed will be changed or gone forever."

New Guineans gather to watch Penn at work in ▶ his portable studio, set up among thatched huts on a fairground. While the studio was being erected an onlooker remarked, "Short fella house him come up long fella," as the frame of fitted pipes and joints rose swiftly into a structure 11 feet high over a 10-by-18-foot floor. Two men can set up the tent, which is light enough to ride on a jeep roof because its frame is aluminum and its covering is nylon. The light is controlled by adjusting the flaps and by the mobile reflector canted in the foreground. Penn's commitment to the studio setting does not extend to such standard studio gear as the view camera. His expedition pictures are shot with 2¼ x 2¼ twin-lens reflexes; he packs five of them and several sets of auxiliary close-up lenses.

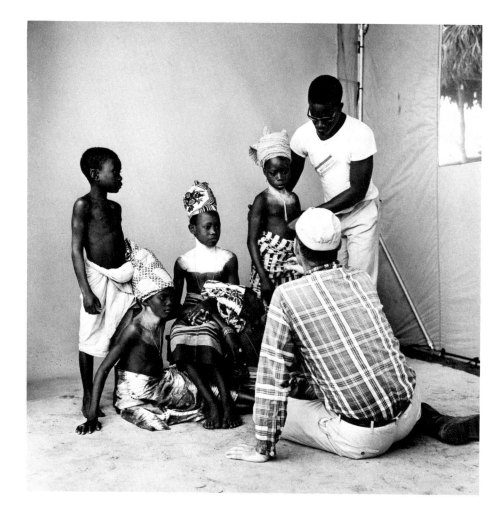

Seated on the floor inside his portable studio, Penn positions Aizo children for a picture (left). The bare tent contains nothing familiar—not even a grass blade for toes to pluck—to distract his sitters. While an assistant interprets his instructions, the youngsters' attention is riveted on Penn; they are spellbound by his intense concentration. With similar single-mindedness he also arranged Aizo market girls, opposite, in a pattern of graceful feminine self-assurance and Asaro tribesmen (overleaf) in threatening poses that recall their ancient traditions of warfare.

Girls of Dahomey tribes like the Aizo, whose ancestors lived near the slave-trade port of Whydah, have long worn a behavioral disguise to protect their privacy from Europeans: they put on false airs of playful gaiety when outsiders are around. Penn overcame this psychological barrier, inimical to his plan to find the real nature of his subjects, by initiating a courteous, formal exchange of greetings and compliments.

Impressed by Penn's diplomacy, the villagers dropped their masks. They became, as Penn put it, "completely available," ready to take a personal part in the magical world within his studio. On its neutral ground they emerged as their real selves, human beings possessed of innate dignity (opposite).

An observance of protocol and the isolation of the studio helped Penn in New Guinea, too. Once, encountering a delay on a trip to photograph the tribesmen of an isolated village, he had a formal apology for his lateness sent ahead to the highlanders who expected him. Evidently touched by this gesture, they willingly posed for him when he showed up. In one portrait (overleaf) the tribesmen, mud-daubed to honor an old victory, affect frightening attitudes through posture and by means of their ceremonial masks. □

IRVING PENN: *Dahomey, Five Girls*, 1967

IRVING PENN: *Asaro Mudmen, New Guinea,* 1970

Focusing on Fashion

4

EDWARD STEICHEN: *An early fashion photograph of a dress by designer Paul Poiret, Paris,* 1911

The High Art of Picturing Style

One of the paradoxes of studio photography is its most glamorous specialty: fashion. The pictures, at their best, are technically expert, esthetically valid and in some cases so beautiful that they are cherished among the finest examples of photographic art. Their appearance in print commands such great attention that fashion assignments attract the best photographers.

Yet fashion photography is as ephemeral as a woman's whim. Its subject matter is severely limited: it consists, amid whatever props, of a model wearing a stylish outfit. The photographer's problem is somehow to give freshness and variety to pictures that, as Edward Steichen *(pages 105, 110-111)* has said, "tell the same story year after year. All he has to present are photographs of the newest fashions." It is hardly a simple problem.

As for the purpose of fashion photography, it may seem simple—a selling job, to put it crassly—but in fact it is actually quite complex. It is the same multiple purpose that is served by the fashion magazines themselves: for one thing, to go out into the dream world of "beautiful people"—the modish and sophisticated, nice-smelling and certainly well-off—and to report back to less-favored people what these trend-setters are wearing, how they are eating, what they are reading, where they are congregating. The purpose goes deeper: to use this "in" world to influence the way ordinary people live, to trade them up from Miami Beach vacations to Montego Bay, from beef stew to beef Wellington—and in the process, to create an atmosphere that will induce readers to buy what is advertised in the magazines, and to dress, even by sew-it-yourself means, after the fashion of the fashion models.

The photographer has several people looking over his shoulder to remind him of this: the dress or accessory designer, the manufacturer, and—since all fashion photographs are meant for publication—a fashion editor and an art director. They help, but it is his imagination, more than proficiency, that is his trustiest weapon. Combined with his innate taste, it enables him to do his job, as defined by Cecil Beaton *(pages 114-115):* "The dressmaker provides the dress, but the photographer must make the woman in that dress appear in a manner that will give all other women a feeling of covetousness."

What often makes women covetous is the sight of another woman inhabiting that desirable world of well-heeled luxury. Some of the most successful photographers of the 1920s and 1930s were aided in creating such a world pictorially by their own real-life familiarity with it. There was Beaton, son of a British timber merchant, who went from the best schools (Harrow and Cambridge) into the top strata of London society, where he indulged twin tastes for party-going and dressing up: he once eschewed conventional dress to appear in a different fancy-costume disguise every day for 10 days. There was the pioneer Gayne de Meyer *(pages 108-109),* whose wife reportedly was the illegitimate daughter of Edward VII and who had a Venetian palace, a London town house and a home in the south of England, all rumored to be provided by his royal connection. De Meyer was a stoutish, cane-sporting exotic: he slept under a blanket of mink and protected his blue-dyed hair with a net while working in the studio. There was George Hoyningen-Huene *(pages 112-113);* he rarely used his title of baron and cultivated left-wing friends, but he also kept a picture of his father, a Baltic nobleman, in full regalia preceding the Czar in the 1896 coronation procession in Moscow. Huene had a fabled temperament: when he was working for *Vogue,* the magazine's art director Mehemed Fehmy Agha, acting on orders, took him to lunch one day and gently suggested that he "behave." Huene upset the table, food and all, right into Agha's lap, ran to the restaurant's telephone booth and called *Harper's Bazaar,* which hired him on the spot. (Agha, a colorful personality in his own right, was the Ukrainian-born son of a Turkish landowner and tobacco grower. A witty raconteur, he was credited with finally laying to rest certain fashion-photography clichés from the De Meyer days by deriding them in a 1939 memo to *Vogue* President Condé Nast: "To be alluring, a model must clutch her hips; to be glamorous, she must lean over backwards; to be dramatic, she must clutch a drape.")

The personal flamboyance of those older photographers has given way before the no-nonsense breed of studio men who produce the fashion shots of the 1970s *(pages 130-140).* The work of this new breed shows a wider variety of influences—social, esthetic and moral. If there is one constant that typifies their generation, it is something quite different from the earlier tendency to make the woman of fashion photographs a passive and overindulged daughter of privileged society. Today's practitioners are apt to try to illuminate some aspect of the inner life of the model, whom they see as a complex human being rather than a decorative clothes hanger. Many of them hope the picture will make a statement about the modern woman's psyche and her role in contemporary life—an ambition that perhaps reflects the anxiety of a world whose values are being challenged as never before.

The problems inherent in fashion photography—the narrowness of its subject matter, its make-believe milieu, its commercial aspect, the plethora of patrons whom it must please—have stimulated some of the world's most gifted photographers in the half century in which it has developed into a specialty. Beautiful clothes and models can provide inspiration, but the photographer must have the talent, skill and patience to work out a style so individualized that his work can be identified at a glance. The pictures on the pages that follow bear the photographers' signature as surely as if they had written their names on the negatives. In meeting their own exacting standards, they have also established fashion photography—whatever its humble origins as the appendage of an industry—as an art in its own right.

De Meyer: Mannered Chic

Prior to World War I the clothes shown in fashion magazines were most often sketched with pen and ink. But in 1913 Condé Nast, then the new publisher of *Vogue* magazine, asked a dilettante photographer whose work he liked to try his hand at photographing fashions. The man was Gayne de Meyer, a Parisian of German ancestry who called himself a baron although his claim to the title was dubious. De Meyer became the pioneer who founded the profession of fashion photography. His success was based on his familiarity with the fashionable world of his time and his ability to interpret it pictorially, and on the ethereal quality of his photographs—which effect he got by veiling his lens with silk gauze and using soft backlighting.

When he died in modest circumstances in Los Angeles in 1946, De Meyer's style had long been passé. It had been superseded by a series of newer trends in fashion photography set by a small group of talented men and women. Each presented a very personal image of the world of fashion and the handsome women who inhabit it —and in doing so molded fashion itself and influenced all studio photography.

This study of a woman in a gold lamé costume was made by De Meyer in Europe, a few years before he came to the United States. Although not strictly a fashion photograph, it was the kind of deliberately blurred image of a richly gowned, glamorous female that led Condé Nast to hire De Meyer to photograph fashion for Vogue.

DE MEYER: *Woman with Cup, c. 1910*

De Meyer almost invariably posed his models standing with one hand firmly on hip, a stance that presumably spelled chic to the baron. At top left the actress Jeanne Eagels in an evening gown and, below, a male model showing off the latest in morning coats both strike the classic De Meyer attitude. At lower left the model's outfit is overwhelmed by her surroundings; De Meyer was also an interior decorator who often created luxurious settings for his fashion shots. Some of Vogue's wealthier readers were so taken with these ornate and exotic backgrounds that they commissioned him to create salons for their town houses.

DE MEYER: *Jeanne Eagels*, 1921

DE MEYER: *Woman with Oriental Plant*, date unknown

DE MEYER: *Male Fashion*, date unknown

Steichen: Master of Lighting

Edward Steichen concluded that when a woman saw a picture of a dress she should get "a very good idea of how it was put together and what it looked like." His decision to take photographs that would make crystal clear the fabric, cut and details of a costume resulted in a forthright style that broke with his predecessors' fussy romanticism.

It also led Steichen to embark on a long and intensive experimentation with lighting. He had been taking fashion photographs as early as 1911, and yet by 1923, when he was doing fashion photography for *Vogue,* he had never made indoor pictures with artificial light. Confronted by the studio electrician's insistence that he use a dozen klieg arc lamps to photograph his first dress for *Vogue,* Steichen took a four-ply thickness of bed sheets and draped it over the entire battery to make the light from the arc lamps appear to be natural illumination (his action moved the electrician to observe, "That guy knows his stuff"). But Steichen soon realized that electric light would be invaluable in giving variety as well as clarity to fashion pictures and began adding lights one at a time until, by the end of his years with *Vogue,* there were, in his own words, "lights going all over the place."

In the photograph at right, one of a series Steichen made beginning in 1924, he used a celebrated model, Marion Morehouse (later wife of the poet e.e. cummings), but set her against a plain background and in a simple composition that focused attention on her dress. Even when he used an absurd prop like the horse on the opposite page, Steichen aimed so many lights at the models, the horse and the reflecting white-tile backdrop that the emphasis was still on the lines of the white fashions themselves.

EDWARD STEICHEN: *Marion Morehouse,* 1927

EDWARD STEICHEN: *White Fashions*, 1935

Hoyningen-Huene: The Classic Ideal

GEORGE HOYNINGEN-HUENE: *Housecoat by Chanel,* 1931

During more than two decades as a fashion photographer, George Hoyningen-Huene refined a style that combined a personal fascination with femininity and a reverence for the art of ancient Western civilization. The son of a Baltic baron and his American wife, Huene (rhymes with "learner") had received a classical esthetic education growing up in the pre-Revolutionary Russian court of Czar Nicholas II. It was a world, as he said in later life, where "men were men and women were women—modern people seem so androgynous to me." To capture the feminine mystique he recalled from his childhood, Huene worked patiently with his models, encouraging them until he had "made them conscious of their femininity . . . and they looked as if they were about to be kissed."

The quality that he strove to bring out in photography had been best portrayed, he felt, by the ancient Greek sculptors' idealizations of female serenity. In his own most characteristic pictures, there was a sense of statuesque monumentality, humanized by the model's air of sweet tranquillity. She seemed a flesh-and-blood Grecian deity—an irresistible image that women sought to make their own by wearing clothes like those that hung so gracefully on Huene's poised figures.

"Texture, line, simplicity—these were the things he liked, the classic truth," said Katharine Hepburn of her friend Huene when he died in 1968. Here he emphasized texture and line by covering the pillars flanking the model with sheet metal and bouncing front spotlights off them, thus dramatizing the shimmering satin-lamé material of the simply cut robe.

The plaster torso in the background of this picture of a clinging crepe gown is almost a Huene trademark. His follower Cecil Beaton (overleaf) noted that Huene's absorption in classic art led him "to bring a whole new collection of properties to his studio: women were posed against Corinthian columns, casts of Hellenic horses, heads of Greek gods."

GEORGE HOYNINGEN-HUENE: *Evening Gown*, 1934

Beaton: Borrowing from the Stage

CECIL BEATON: *Evening Gown,* 1934

The fashion photography of Cecil Beaton foretold the renown he was later to gain as a stage and screen designer (of sets and costumes for the play *Coco* and the movie *My Fair Lady,* among others). His photographs, executed mostly in the 1930s, are stage productions in microcosm, featuring sets designed by Beaton (who also frequently painted them) and lighting that mimicked the spotlights of the Broadway and Piccadilly shows of the period. But, despite the theatricality, Beaton pursued the realistic tradition: the clothes and the accessories were always as much stage center as the model.

Often the model was a well-known actress. Beaton was one of the first photographers to sense that stage and screen stars were desirable mannequins—their strong personalities enhanced the clothes they wore, and their well-publicized glamor aided in popularizing fashions.

A fast worker—he averaged 60 exposures during a two-hour sitting—Beaton was at the time somewhat self-consciously uninterested in technical procedure. He once said that he was "ashamed at being so inept at the technical side of the game," but he also rather enjoyed the amazed reaction of his listeners when he let it be known that he had taken his first pictures for *Vogue* with a hand-held, pocket-sized, folding Kodak No. 3A that was precariously set on a rickety old tripod.

Beaton staged the tableau at left by placing three models behind a backlighted, translucent screen of white muslin to produce the shadow silhouettes of a flower woman (left) and two beaux offering violets to a puppet-goddess of the haut monde arrayed in a costly formal gown.

CECIL BEATON: *Spring Fashion*, 1949

A favorite Beaton device was to "embower" his models in mixed real and artificial flowers. Above, he used it to create a Vogue cover by having the model put her head through a hole in a canvas that he had decorated.

Beaton produced a series of "playlets"; this one (right) starred the comedienne Ilka Chase as a jilted girl. Hopefully the unhappy ending would not deter women from buying the Henri Bendel gown and Tiffany jewelry she was wearing.

CECIL BEATON: *The Florist's Box*, 1937

Man Ray: Experimenting with Patterns

MAN RAY: *Gown by Schiaparelli, 1935*

Man Ray, a devotee of the iconoclastic artistic movement known as Dadaism, brought its ideas to the pages of high-style magazines. A fashion photographer from 1921 to the early 1940s, Man Ray was perfectly capable of executing relatively conventional pictures *(left)* of a suitably romantic nature. More often he used specialized darkroom techniques—many of them conceived by Man Ray himself—in creating photographs the like of which had never appeared on the fashion scene.

Man Ray would tilt his easel when enlarging a picture to create a startlingly elongated silhouette of model and costume or, using the technique known as solarization, expose a partly processed picture to reverse some tones, black for white and white for black. Man Ray's farthest-out innovation was something he called the "Rayograph"—a picture like the one opposite, made in the darkroom by placing various objects on a piece of printing paper and briefly exposing both to light. Such shadow pictures were not original with Man Ray, but the abstractions he created in them produced a surrealistic chic.

The Hindu-inspired dress at left was designed by Elsa Schiaparelli. For this picture, taken at the 1935 Paris showings, Ray avoided his intricate innovations. The picture was to be radioed to New York, a practice followed by Vogue and Harper's Bazaar. Man Ray realized that the infant art of radiophotography, with its observable scanning lines, would itself produce an unusual picture.

Man Ray made one of his celebrated Rayographs ▶ to convey an impression of the new fashions coming over the radio waves. This Rayograph, used in Bazaar, was produced by placing a cutout elongated silhouette of a model and a piece of the loosely woven material of her gown atop a piece of printing paper. The material's honeycomb effect suggested a radiophoto's lines.

MAN RAY: *Fashion Rayograph,* 1934

Munkacsi: The Drama of the Outdoors

MARTIN MUNKACSI: *Beach Fashion*, 1936

When Martin Munkacsi arrived in the United States in 1934, he had been the highest-paid news photographer both in his native Hungary and later in Germany. Engaged at *Harper's Bazaar* by a new editor who gave him a free hand, though she knew he had not done fashion work, Munkacsi startled competitors with his first picture.

For a bathing-suit feature he took his model out of the studio to a windy Long Island beach, and insisted that she run toward him. Such action poses had never been used for fashion, and Munkacsi's pictures were tartly dismissed by *Vogue's* chief editor as "farm girls jumping over fences." Yet the image he created of the American woman swinging into splendid action out of doors became an enduring rival to the pampered creature who had adorned earlier fashion photography.

Her boldly striped beach coat billowing behind her, Munkacsi's model strides into the wind—a good illustration of his advice, published in Harper's Bazaar in 1935: "Never pose your subjects. Let them move about naturally. Don't let the girl stop to put her hair to rights."

A brave model perched on a parapet of a ▶ futuristic building at the 1939 New York World's Fair holds on to the wall with one hand as Munkacsi records his arresting view of a winter outfit (right). He once persuaded a reluctant model to sit on the back of a live camel by taunting her with the epithet "Supercoward!"

MARTIN MUNKACSI: *For the Winter Season*, 1939

Frissell: Playclothes in Faraway Places

Photographing fashion out of doors became a dominant trend during the late 1930s and into the 1940s as more and more women entered the active world outside the home. The sportswoman was a new female idol and to keep her free and easy, the fashion industry brought out bigger and better lines of sports- and playclothes. The outstanding photographer of outdoor wear was a young society woman named Toni Frissell, who preferred to shoot on location because she was "never mechanically minded" enough to feel at ease among the lights and equipment of the studio. But she had received good training on how to take pictures out of doors from her brother Varick, who had been a newsreel cameraman before his early death.

Besides her own talent, Miss Frissell brought two other advantages to the growing fad for sporty fashion photography: an ardent sportswoman herself (on an assignment, she once worked out with the United States Olympic ski team), she knew how to pose her athletic models convincingly, and how best to display the functional nature of their riding habits or tennis dresses.

Moreover, as a fully accredited Manhattan social registerite, she was able to take her models into exclusive watering places of the rich, such as Bailey's Beach in Newport or Cypress Point in California *(opposite)*. When *Vogue* or *Harper's Bazaar* subscribers examined a playdress photographed in such sacrosanct settings, their urge to acquire it was presumably strengthened.

TONI FRISSELL: *Bikini*, 1946

An alert Harper's Bazaar editor, spotting her first bikini on the French Riviera in 1946, sensed its imminent popularity and assigned Toni Frissell to picture it. Miss Frissell transported a model and a bikini to fashionable Montego Bay, Jamaica, and arranged the model on the sand at an hour when the sun would cast shadows long and dramatic enough to emphasize the contours of the girl's body. Result: the first picture of a bikini to be seen in a U.S. magazine.

Offering her face to the sun and the wind, a model in a characteristic Frissell pose shows off what was described as "the summer uniform of the land," a shirtwaist dress. The setting is a beach resort at Del Monte, California, where the sports-loving rich disported themselves amid surrealistic cypress trees and barking seals.

TONI FRISSELL: *Shirtwaist,* 1938

Mrs. Wolfe used Kodachrome film in an 8 x 10 view camera to record the delicate hues of this photograph. To set off the old-fashioned charm of the lace-trimmed nightgown that is the focal point of the picture, she employed the Victorian setting of her own New Jersey bedroom. A decorator like Gayne de Meyer (pages 108-109), Mrs. Wolfe followed the studio-photographer's tradition, not only choosing film and arranging lighting, but selecting all the props for her set.

LOUISE DAHL-WOLFE: *My Bedroom,* 1942

Dahl-Wolfe: A Sense of Color and Setting

LOUISE DAHL-WOLFE: *Sun Fashion, 1952*

Louise Dahl-Wolfe was a painter and decorator turned photographer, with an intense interest in color that led her to pioneer its use in fashion pictures. In the 1930s, when she started taking fashion pictures, black-and-white was thought preferable for this medium because even slight deviations from the true colors of the fashions could cause the photograph to be rejected. Though Kodachrome, the first modern color film, became available after 1935, it could not always be counted on to produce true colors, in or out of doors. Mrs. Wolfe worked under strong klieg lights in the studio, using huge one-shot cameras *(page 58)*. She trained herself with diligence, absorbing all she could from camera technicians and engravers, and by the time she retired from the field in 1962, she had contributed such "firsts" as the atmospheric photograph on the opposite page. It is perhaps the earliest color fashion photograph to use interior natural light, a difficult achievement during this period of still-erratic film.

After World War II, Mrs. Wolfe helped introduce another innovation by taking her models to little-known spots almost anywhere on earth and photographing them against such exotic settings as the ruins of ancient civilizations *(left)*. The effect was to add another dimension to the image of the outdoor girl Munkacsi and Frissell had glorified, by making her a citizen of the world.

Photographer and model traveled to the Maya ruins in Mexico's Yucatán peninsula to make this picture of smartly matched shorts and top posed against a stone where human sacrifices had been offered to propitiate the gods.

Horst: Highlighting the Sitter

German-born H. P. Horst, known professionally simply as Horst, created techniques of lighting that were, in the words of *Vogue* art director Mehemed Fehmy Agha, "what the lighting of sculpture in museums should be: three-dimensional and dramatic." To get the three-dimensional effect, Horst placed light sources above and diagonal to the model to slant a pattern of light and shadow downward across each side of her figure, creating dramatically accented shots like that of the noted couturière "Coco" Chanel at right. (Another of Horst's many lighting methods was less popular with fashion editors: for his so-called black compositions —pictures subtly featuring highlighted models and black backgrounds—he used so few lights that the editors complained at times that the dress was "shrouded in deepest mystery.")

Horst himself feels that the chief problem for a studio photographer is that "almost everybody is camera shy." This forces him to study his own feelings and responses about the sitter to decide on the best way to photograph her. He was not satisfied with his first take of Chanel. He asked her to pose a second time and, while trying to think of the kind of surroundings that would induce ease on her part, remembered a couch he had seen that had belonged to Marie Antoinette; here, Mlle. Chanel gracefully reclines on it.

HORST: *Gabrielle (Coco) Chanel*, 1937

The great dress designer Chanel was photographed in Vogue's Paris studio wearing one of her own creations, a jersey afternoon dress. Horst made it a side-view study to bring out the graceful beauty of her profile and used small frontal light sources focused on the sitter's head to frame her against the background shadows. This picture was the personal favorite of the designer, who died in 1971.

Horst once said: "It's not how many or what kinds ▶ of lights you use, but how they are placed," a technique demonstrated by the coolly elegant picture opposite. Horst backlighted a white sheet with both a flood- and a spotlight and placed his model in the center of the circle of light thrown by the spot. Then, to accent her furs, he lit her from below by placing lights near her feet and hiding them with the curved oval prop in the foreground.

HORST: *Ensemble by Hattie Carnegie*, 1937

IRVING PENN: *Twelve Most-Photographed Models*, 1947

Penn: Cool Elegance

No fashion photographer ever worked harder to bring out the distinctive quality of each of his models than Irving Penn. As the dean of fashion photography in the years after World War II, Penn began his fashion sittings early in the morning. Sometimes, however, it was 5 o'clock in the afternoon before he was satisfied with any of his painfully arrived-at pictures. Once the mannequin was made up and dressed, Penn would ask her to stand against a plain background; then he would study her until he found some trait that he felt might reveal the concept of woman and costume. Such sessions could be grueling for both photographer and model, but they resulted in some memorable images of serenely beautiful young women displaying striking outfits with timeless unconcern *(left)*.

Times changed—and, over two decades, so did Penn. Many of his pictures had been black and whites, severe in mood and strong in form. But as the world of fashion became lighter in feeling, his own style shifted. Now it conveyed more humor, a sense of what he calls "electric prettiness" captured in colorful clothes worn by delectable, smiling—better yet, laughing—models.

Sometimes Penn supercharges the electric prettiness into incandescence. To get this intensity into pictures, he works rapidly, with complete concentration and with no waste motion. The model spends seven eighths of her time in the hands of hairdresser, stylist, make-up man, and only one eighth in front of Penn's camera while electronic flashes pop at disconcerting speed. She has no time to get tired of posing —and if all goes well, the pictures come out flower fresh.

IRVING PENN: *Girl in Black and White*, 1950

Penn's picture of Jean Patchet, a famous model of the 1950s, was the first black and white specially commissioned to replace the color illustrations Vogue had used on its cover since 1909. The symmetry is broken only by the model's sidelong glance. To help get the contrasts Penn wanted, she used black lipstick, improvised from mascara.

◄ Penn's tribute to his co-workers, the intricately posed group portrait (left) of the top models of the 1940s, reflects personal quirks: he preferred that his models wear gloves—here eight of the 12 do so—and, at least, no nail polish. Lisa Fonssagrives (seated, in profile, sixth from left), whom he met at this sitting, later became Mrs. Penn.

Avedon: Emphasizing the Bizarre

RICHARD AVEDON: *Dress by Paco Rabane, 1967*

Richard Avedon's fashion photographs often exploit the excitement generated by headline-making events, personalities or trends. For *Vogue's* coverage of the 1962 Paris collections, he photographed a 10-page spoof of the scrambling courtship of movie stars Elizabeth Taylor and Richard Burton, who were then dashing around Europe pursued by an avid press corps. Dressed in the new fashions, Suzy Parker, the decade's most famous model, played the role of Miss Taylor; the actor-director Mike Nichols was the male lead.

Avedon has an instinct for matching the model to the moment. In the mid-1960s, when blacks were beginning to appear in television commercials and in fashion pictures, he was first to work with an overwhelmingly exotic, six-foot-two girl, Donyale Luna *(left),* who rapidly became the most photographed black model in fashion. And in 1968, struck by the oddly wide-set features of a society teenager named Penelope Tree *(opposite),* Avedon persuaded her to pose for him. Modeling eclectic African, gypsy, American-Indian, space-suit styles worn by the young as the decade closed, Miss Tree became an image of the liberated generation. ☐

Looking ultimately avant-garde, model Donyale Luna (left) carried off the futuristic design of what Vogue described as a "mini-modern-gladiator dress," made of squares of aluminum hinged together. She wore sandals with thigh-high thongs to complete the outfit.

Penelope Tree's broad cheekbones are encased ▶ in the silver bands of an African-inspired mask (opposite). Avedon achieved the startled-fawn look of this picture by panning his camera across Miss Tree's face as a strobe flashed at 1/20,000 second, slightly blurring her features.

RICHARD AVEDON: *Mask by Emanuel Ungaro,* 1968

Celebrating Today's World

The fashion photographers of the 1970s often borrow techniques from various styles of modern art: Impressionism, Symbolism, Surrealism, even Cubism *(pages 131-135).* Like the painters who first developed these techniques, the photographers who adapted them to fashion work in the 1960s became embroiled in controversy. Late in 1965, Norman Norell, a top United States designer, expressed the annoyance of his fellow couturiers: "Fashion photographers have really gotten out of hand. They distort a suit or dress beyond recognition." His well-known colleague James Galanos agreed: "The important point of fashion is too often lost because the photographer gets involved in the model or the scene he is shooting —everything but the dress."

Fortunately for the photographers, the fashion editors tended to side with them. The fashion director of *Harper's Bazaar* thought the complaints "come from designers who are older and not with it." *Vogue's* editorial director said, "Though some of them undoubtedly prefer the . . . conventional photograph, most designers are happy to be part of an avant-garde development."

The acceptance of some distortion in fashion photographs enabled the photographers to give their work a really contemporary look. And that, according to Bert Stern, is where it's all at. "The photographer has to respond to today," he says. "If he doesn't, he's getting himself ready to be obsolete." For Stern this response can take the form of a pictorial comment on technology and its effects on society *(pages 136-137).* For Hiro, borrowing a leaf from the book of his mentor Richard Avedon *(page 128),* it may involve using "contemporary models for the contemporary focus": discovering, for example, the striking women to be found in such previously unfashionable societies as Puerto Ricans in the East or *chicanos* in the West. Hiro is also intrigued by the space age: his contract with *Harper's Bazaar* stipulates that he will be the first fashion photographer the magazine sends to the moon.

The fashion photographer of the '70s reflects trends in contemporary life in a way that would sadly perplex his professional ancestor, Gayne de Meyer. He photographs fashion accessories so that they seem to loom larger than life *(pages 134-135)* because for many hell-bent consumers such goods really do have grotesquely immense importance. He makes his pictures more explicitly sexy *(pages 138-139)* because the climate of today's world is sexually liberated. He has created an image of an existence *(page 140)* that is concerned more with a down-to-earth life style and the clothes that are appropriate to it, than with the elusive fantasies of leisured elegance for the few.

During their Cubist phases Pablo Picasso and ▶ Georges Braque, following Cubism's practice of breaking up a subject into many facets, painted portraits that showed their subjects from several viewpoints. Mel Sokolsky used the same idea when he was commissioned to make a photograph (opposite) illustrating eye and lip make-up. The usual method of creating multiple-image pictures is to place one negative on top of another and print them on the same sheet. The problem is that the photographer does not actually see the images in combination until the print is developed. Sokolsky wanted to exert control over his design from the beginning, so he placed an earlier-made slide showing the model's profile in a projector and threw its image on her features as she sat facing him. He used the projector's zoom lens to adjust image size until he got exactly the effect he wanted and then snapped the shutter on his 35mm Canonflex. He floodlit the wall behind the model with very bright light to wash out that portion of the projected profile-image that otherwise would have spilled over onto the left-hand background. His two-faced image is a useful fashion shot because it offers a double display of the effect of the make-up; but Sokolsky says that, like the Cubist painters and others before them, he was also using the double image to comment on the dual nature of every woman's inner self.

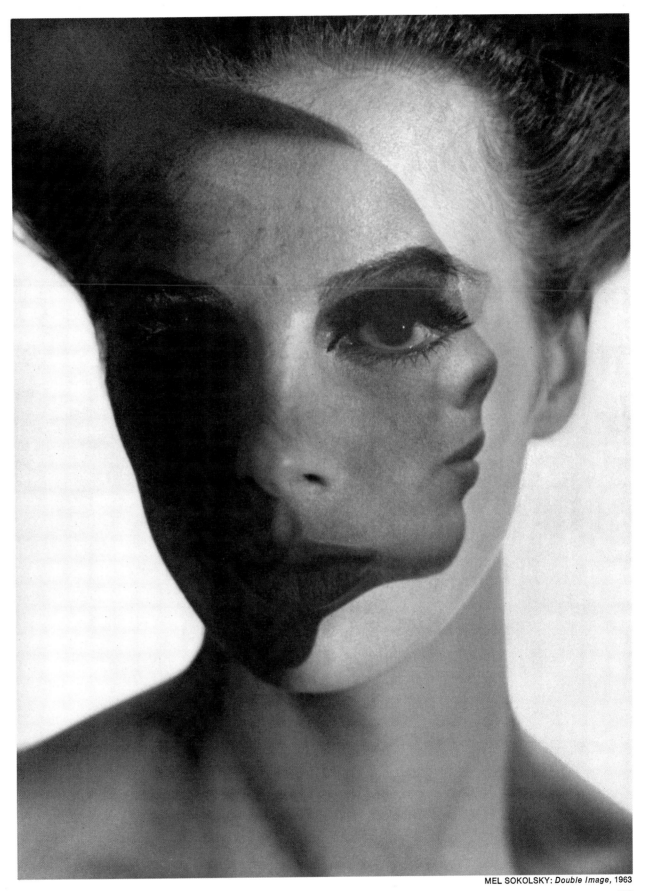

MEL SOKOLSKY: *Double Image*, 1963

Employing the Element of Shock

HIRO: *High-Fashion Fabrics,* 1967

The French, as usual, had a phrase: *épater le bourgeois* ("to astound the bourgeois"), and it described the shock felt by the public in the late 19th and early 20th Centuries on first viewing the work of the artistic schools known as Impressionism and Cubism. The Cubists' distorted perspectives, shattering the tradition that a painting should faithfully mirror its subject and never call attention to itself, profoundly bewildered viewers. Equally disturbing was the painters' bizarre juxtaposition of dissimilar objects, such as Juan Gris's guitar with snow-capped mountains. Today fashion photographer Hiro (real name: Yesuhiro Wakabayashi) employs freakish perspective *(left)* to produce the same sense of shock. And Art Kane says the animal symbols in his fashion shots *(right)* are there to "say something about the nature of the woman in the picture as a human being"—which is the explanation offered by the post-Impressionist Paul Gauguin for the inclusion of strange animal-specters that haunt the girls in his Tahitian canvases.

To contrast the vivid patterns of the dress materials at left, Hiro created an eye-deceiving design whose flat perspective all but hides its components: two models sit back to back on the floor, with a third girl straddling the shoulders of one of the seated girls. Perched on a platform above, Hiro aimed his Nikon down on the group.

Commissioned by the British magazine Queen to shoot some Anglo-American fashions available both in New York and in London, Art Kane used the theme of "the inner life of the young woman of Manhattan" as a motif to tie his pictures together. In the one at right, his model, clad in a petal-skirted chiffon evening dress with waist-plunging décolletage, sits in an empty city apartment, alongside a live boa constrictor. The snake was intended to symbolize the threat of loneliness that Kane sees menacing the outwardly elegant, yet essentially isolated, New York career girl.

ART KANE: *New York Woman*, 1970

Glorifying the Object

SILANO: *Handbag, 1967*

The tendency of an affluent society to glorify its goods is nicely exemplified in the photographs of William Silano. He likes to take pictures of inanimate objects that present them as substantial, even monumental, images. Moving in close to his subject and shooting from an angle slightly below it, he gives fashion accessories gigantic proportions that vastly increase their impressiveness. He also favors surrealistic color and lighting effects: he believes that by creating a mystery and "tension" between the object and its surroundings, he endows it with a pictorial life of its own. At his most successful, Silano transforms commercial products into colossal images that all but command materialists to worship them.

Silano took the photograph of a handbag at left from a distance of two or three feet, standing on the roof of his New York City studio. He perched the bag on a ledge covered with brown seamless paper and placed a small mirror so that it reflected the light from the noonday sun (visible just behind the bag, on the left) onto the front of the bag. Angle and lighting were planned to make the bag seem to be a gargantuan object looming on the horizon against the light of dawn.

The ski boot opposite was photographed on the ▶ shore of Long Island Sound. It was a summer afternoon, so Silano simulated ice on the ground by melting a quarter-inch-thick sheet of clear plastic, on which he set the boot. To give the landscape its unnatural yet provocative colors, Silano shot his picture on infrared film.

SILANO: *Ski Boot*, 1967

Style for a Dehumanized Society

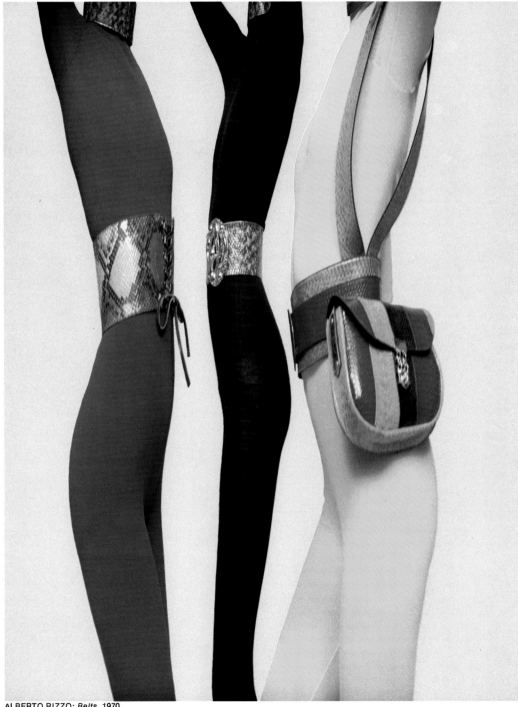

ALBERTO RIZZO: *Belts*, 1970

Bert Stern took the picture opposite at the Paris showing of André Courrèges's 1969 collection. Stern likes the designer's tendency to bare the body because he believes that the physical presence of the human being should be stressed in the face of the menace of the machine. Here he wanted to make the models in their microdresses appear to be pitting their flesh—however pitiably —against the threatening forces in today's technological environment. So he posed them marching in lock step like so many robots.

On the other hand, when Alberto Rizzo was commissioned to photograph fashions in belts, he created deliberately depersonalized images *(left).* To dehumanize his models he dressed them in the anonymity of leotards, posed them against an aseptic white background and aimed his camera to crop any individualizing features, such as heads, legs or arms.

To elongate the models' torsos (left), Alberto Rizzo shot his picture with an anamorphic lens. Such lenses compress one dimension of an image but leave the other dimension unchanged. Here he adjusted the lens to squeeze the horizontal image into snakelike lengthiness.

*Stern used Courrèges's own showroom ►
mannequins instead of photographic models in
the picture opposite because they knew how
to move, and motion was important to the concept
of his picture. Since their faces were not as
conventionally photogenic as those of
photographic models, he partially obscured their
features with Courrèges-designed Dynel wigs.*

BERT STERN: *Metal Dresses*, 1969

Sex in the Seventies

The picture at right appeared in the August 15, 1963, issue of *Vogue.* The model's bare bosom was implied rather than flaunted. Nevertheless, the photograph marked the advent of the sexual revolution of the '60s, a phenomenon that caused a new freedom in fashion and its photography. Thereafter bras dropped, as *Vogue* put it, "like autumn leaves," and pictures of the topless monokini replaced the bikini in the pages of the magazine, accompanied by advice to readers on how to be "seen proudly uncovered." Ultimately, *Vogue* got around to a stylish version of a *Playboy* magazine staple: a centerfold, double-truck nude girl; she was photographed by Irving Penn.

Men got into the act in 1968, when the French fashion journal *Elle* published a head-on photograph of a male nude, in an ad for underwear. The next step was to bring men and women together in fashion pictures, with the male model presented not as the admiring background figure of the past but in a more candidly sexual role. By the start of the '70s, men and women were exhibiting togetherness in high-fashion photographs, clothed to be sure, but often intertwined *(opposite).*

To photograph an example of the heavy, textured hosiery that was then the latest thing (right), Art Kane took advantage of the new sexual freedom to create a scene suggesting an elegant, European-type brothel, and presented his model as an infinitely more accessible type than the old-style untouchable mannequin. And the German photographer H. P. Mühlemann, assigned to illustrate the desirable flexibility of synthetic-fiber knitwear, draped his models in a tenderly intimate pose (opposite) of slightly understated eroticism.

ART KANE: *Girl in Blue Stockings,* 1963

H. P. MÜHLEMANN: *Medico's Boutique Fashions*. 1970

A Turn to Realism

The kind of glamor synthesized by others in the field of fashion photography is gone from the picture at right by Alen MacWeeney. So is the assumption that in fashion the world is always happy and bright: it is a gray day and rain beats against the windowpane. Mac-Weeney feels that to survive as an art form, fashion photography will reach closer to reality in its reportage: a record of what real-life men and women will wear while pursuing their daily routines in their ordinary surroundings. The photographer will get his best effects by shooting on location, choosing sites that are accessible or familiar to the public to give his backgrounds the force of authenticity. He will use non-professional models, people who are fat, thin, young, old, sleek or dowdy —anything, as long as they are photographically interesting. His picture may be tinged with social comment, but never tainted with the appeal to snobbish instincts that long characterized much fashion photography. Thus MacWeeney's fashionable world of the 1970s is a relaxed and realistic place where everyone is free to do his own thing. □

Seated on a window ledge at the Chelsea, a venerable Manhattan hotel frequented by artists and writers, a leggy girl in a simply cut minidress kibitzes, ignored by her card-playing boyfriends. She is a far cry from the pampered woman whose regally self-assured presence, photographed against extravagant backgrounds, symbolized the woman of fashion in the past.

ALEN MacWEENEY: *Winter Day,* 1969

A Versatile Studio Tool 5

Inside the Modern View Camera 144

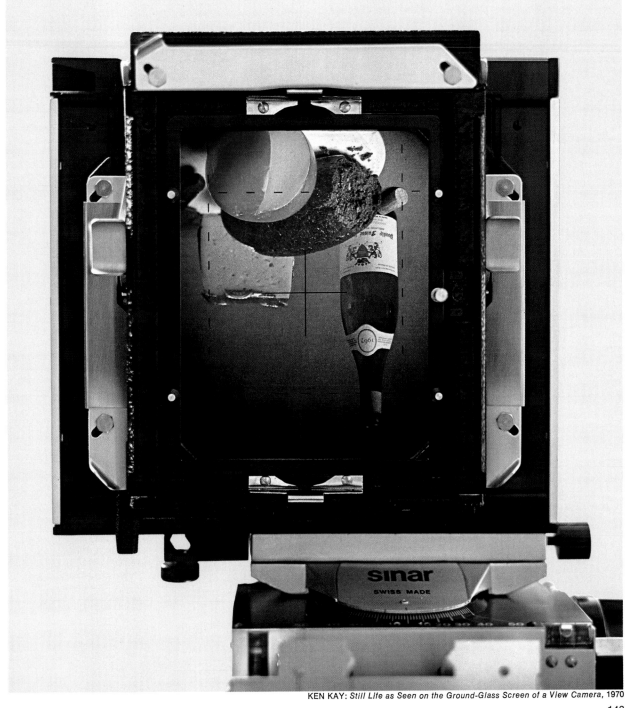

KEN KAY: *Still Life as Seen on the Ground-Glass Screen of a View Camera*, 1970

Inside the Modern View Camera

One of the things that cost money in a high-quality camera is precision. Consider, for example, the relation of film and lens: to ensure sharp overall focus, they must be lined up absolutely parallel, one squarely behind the other. If they are not—if the lens is the least bit out of line or if the film is not held exactly straight behind the lens—the picture will be marred by soft or blurry spots that no amount of careful focusing can possibly eliminate.

What is the purpose, then, of paying a good deal of money (from $100 to $1,500 without lens) for a view camera whose film and lens can be deliberately "unaligned"? Because in trained hands this can make it possible to take pictures that a rigid camera, no matter how expensive, simply cannot produce. An obvious example is trying to photograph a tall building from across the street. Tip the camera up to include the top, and the entire building seems to fall over backward in the finished photograph. If it were possible to lower the film in the back of the camera so that it recorded a different part of the image projected by the lens, then considerably more of the building could be included within the frame of the picture.

This is only one of the adjustments that can be made by the view camera, whose back (film) and front (lens) can be independently twisted and moved in a number of directions: up, down or sideways, tilted forward or back, swiveled to either side. Each of these movements has a different effect on the negative. If properly understood, they can be used to impart an extraordinary amount of discipline and control to photography. They can eliminate or increase distortion; they can straighten up walls, pull things into or out of focus, change perspective. How these movements are accomplished mechanically in a camera is shown in the diagram opposite. What they do photographically is explained on the next 26 pages.

In describing these movements the directions given relate, for consistency and clarity, not to the inverted image shown on the view camera's ground-glass viewing screen, but to the photograph that is actually taken.

Two basic movements that can be made with the front and back of the view camera are loosely known to photographers as swings and tilts. Swings are movements around the *vertical* axis of either lens or film—i.e., when either is twisted to the left or right. Tilts are movements around the *horizontal* axis of lens or film—i.e., when either is tipped forward or backward.

In addition to these two movements, many view cameras provide two others. One is sideways movement of lens or film to either left or right; this is known as shift. The other is raising or lowering of lens or film; this is known as rise or fall. These four movements can be used separately or in combination, according to the practical or esthetic need of the photographer. A camera that provides all of them is the most versatile instrument known to photography.

parts

A | lens
B | aperture scale
C | shutter-speed scale
D | lens board
E | lens-board-adjustment thumbscrew
F | front standard
G | front-standard-adjustment thumbscrew
H | shutter-release cable
J | bellows
K | tripod mount
L | ground glass
M | back-adjustment thumbscrew
N | back
O | back standard
P | back-standard-adjustment thumbscrew
Q | dark slide
R | film holder
S | film sheet

movements

1 | back-rise
2 | back-fall
3 | front-rise
4 | front-fall
5 | back-shift left
6 | back-shift right
7 | front-shift left
8 | front-shift right
9 | back-tilt backward
10 | back-tilt forward
11 | front-tilt backward
12 | front-tilt forward
13 | back-swing left
14 | back-swing right
15 | front-swing left
16 | front-swing right
17 | front focusing
18 | back focusing

This simplified cutaway of a view camera makes ▶ clear its basic relationship to all cameras: it is a box with a lens at one end and a sheet of film at the other. Unlike other cameras, however, the box is not rigid. The front face, to which the lens is fastened, can be moved independently—up or down, tilted forward or back—by loosening a pair of thumbscrews (E). A second pair of thumbscrews (M) permits similar movements of the back. Two other thumbscrews (G and P) permit front or back to be shifted, swung or focused. In addition, different-sized film can be used by substituting film holders and camera-backs that are designed for those sizes. Furthermore, the front end of the camera will accept different lenses, and extra bellows can be inserted between front and back (page 168) to accommodate their different focal lengths and to provide extreme extensions for close-up work. Finally, if the focal length of the lens is so short that the regular bellows cannot be squeezed tight enough, it can be removed, and a special bag bellows substituted (page 158).

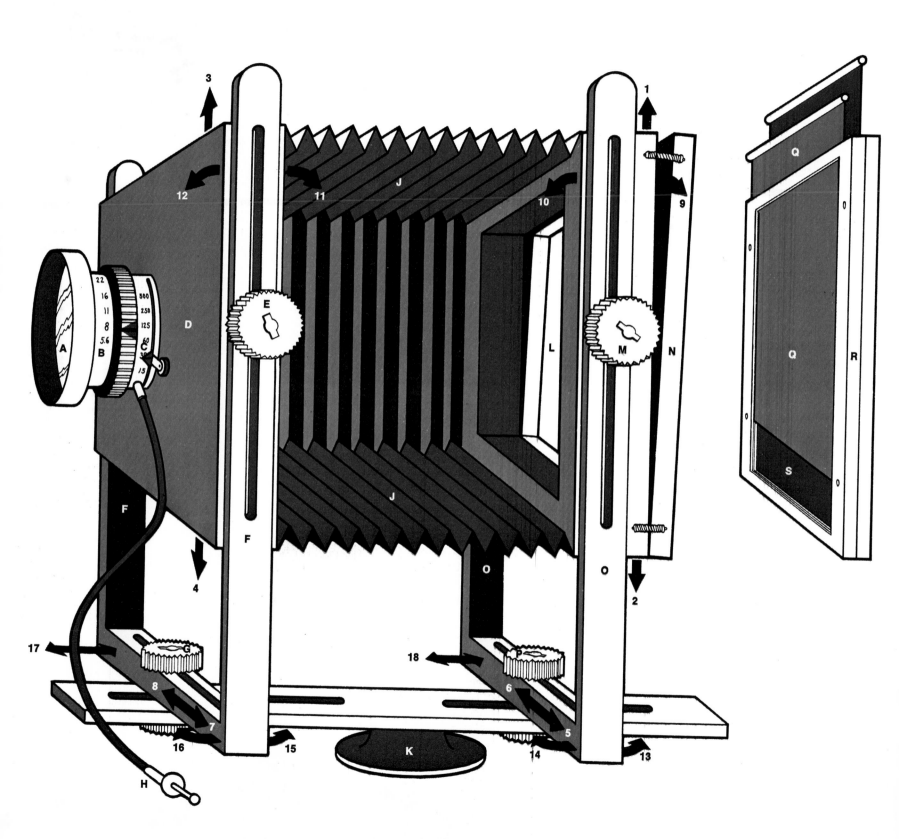

The View Camera's Limitations

Checking focus with a hand-held magnifier, the photographer does not place it squarely on the ground glass because the camera-back has been swung to the left and the lens tilted downward. Instead, he holds the magnifier at an angle to keep it lined up with the incoming light rays.

As a guard against too extreme swings and tilts, this Sinar camera shows a small circle of light at each corner of the ground glass when light coming from lens to film is not blocked by the camera bellows. The user must check the four corners of the ground glass one at a time.

In cameras, as in everything else, one does not get something for nothing. The flexibility that tilts and swings give the view camera comes at the expense of compactness and speed of use. This is a camera for slow, careful work, not for candid shooting. Furthermore, there is a limit beyond which the view camera's parts may not be twisted. Light normally travels in straight lines and if the camera is swung or tilted too far, the bellows will interfere with the light traveling from lens to film. Some cameras have devices to determine whether or not this problem is occurring. At each corner of the ground-glass viewing screen the corner itself has been cut away. Inspection of a corner will show a circle of light when rays are coming from the lens to that corner of the ground glass. If no such circle is visible, then the photographer knows that the bellows is cutting off the light.

Another problem encountered with swings and tilts is focusing. To obtain the extreme sharpness of which the camera is capable, the photographer ordinarily checks focus by placing a magnifier directly on the ground glass. This is easily done if the back and front of the camera are squared off. But if the back is swung at an angle or other adjustments have been made, as in the picture at left, the photographer must hold the magnifier at an angle to the ground glass. Finding the sharp point of focus under these conditions takes some time and some practice.

Finally, though the back of the camera can be used with film of various sizes, and the front with lenses of all types, match-ups must be made with care, or the photographer will obtain results like those shown at right.

The importance of matching film size with the proper lens is shown in these three pictures. Each was taken from the same spot with a camera containing 8 x 10 film, but with three different 135mm lenses designed for different film sizes. You can make a photograph with an 8 x 10 camera using a lens designed for a 2¼ x 2¼ camera, as the first picture shows. However, it is a waste of good film, since the lens can cover only a small section in the middle of the 8 x 10 film sheet.
The same image could have been obtained, at lower film cost, by taking the 8 x 10 back out of the camera and substituting a 2¼ x 2¼ back.

By switching to a lens designed for a larger film size (here, 4 x 5), a much greater part of the 8 x 10 sheet receives an image. Note that the size of the fountain itself has not changed. It cannot; as long as the focal length remains at 135mm, the fountain parts visible in both pictures will be exactly the same size. All that the second lens has done is widen the field of view to include more of the fountain and utilize more of the 8 x 10 film sheet.

With a 135mm lens designed for still larger film, almost the entire film sheet receives the image. This demonstration makes several important points: mismatches cost money in wasted film surface. They also cut down on the swings and tilts possible since, with a mismatch like the one at left, the shaft of light coming from lens to film is already a narrow one. In addition, the relationship between focal length, film size and lens characteristic is revealed. The first picture makes clear that a lens with a focal length of 135mm designed for small-sized film produces a telephoto effect with a narrow field of view. But the same 135mm focal length built to cover 8 x 10 film produces a wide-angle effect.

The Four Camera Movements: 1 | Rise and Fall

To understand the effect each movement has on a negative, one must first look at a picture where no movement has been cranked into any part of the camera, where film and lens are both squarely lined up on an object. This has been done with the cube directly at right. Camera position was centered on the cube. All controls were set at zero. Focus was on the top front edge.

The result is an image that falls in the exact center of the picture frame. The cube's top front edge, being closest to the camera, is the largest. Being the focal point, it is also the sharpest. The two visible surfaces of the cube fall away in size and sharpness at an equal rate. With this "reference" cube as a standard, changes in its shape, sharpness and position—as a result of camera manipulation—can be explained.

The first manipulation is a rise or fall of the camera-back. This is simply an up-and-down movement of the film; it makes no change in the angular relationship of film plane to lens or cube, thus there is no change in the shape of the cube. All that happens when the back is raised (or lowered) is that the image on the film is raised (or lowered). If the front of the camera is moved up or down, the image on the film also moves —but in the opposite direction.

Does it matter whether the front or back is used to move the cube? Yes. Back movement changes only the location of the image, but does not affect its shape. Front movement does affect shape. This effect is too slight to be observed in these pictures, but changes in the relationship between one object and another can be seen if a second object is added to the picture—here, a small post placed in front of the cube.

reference cube

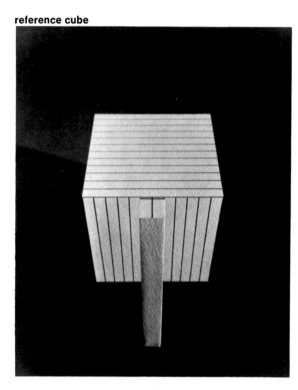

back-rise

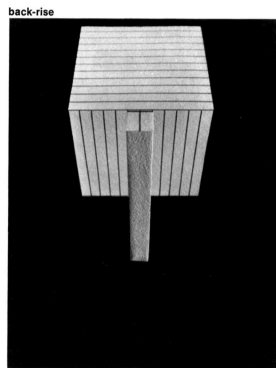

The reference cube was shot with all camera adjustments set at zero position, looking downward, as the diagram shows, from an angle of 45°. This puts the cube in the center of the film, and produces a symmetrical figure. The next four pictures, although they move the cube around on the film through rise and fall of back and lens, apparently make no changes in the shape of the cube's image on the film.

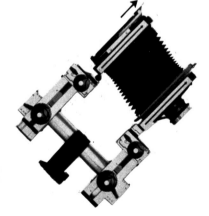

Raising the back of the camera moves the cube higher on the film without changing its shape. Nor does this movement affect the position or shape of the small post that has been centered exactly in front of the cube, with its top in line with the cube's front edge—as comparison with the photograph of the reference cube will show.

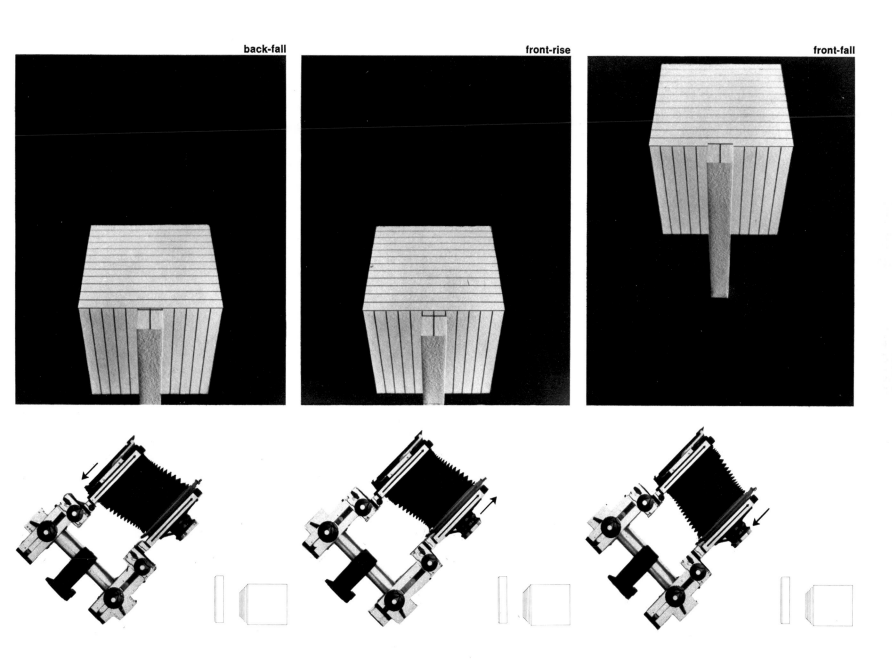

back-fall

front-rise

front-fall

Lowering the back of the camera lowers the position of the cube on the film. Otherwise, as before, there is no change in the shape of the cube or in its relationship with the post. This is because the film, though raised or lowered, is still getting the same image from the lens, which has not moved relative to the cube or post.

Raising the lens lowers the image of the cube on the film. In this its effect is the same as back-fall. However, lens movement causes a change that does not occur with back movement: it affects the relationship between cube and post because the lens is now looking at them from a slightly different position. Compare the apparent height of the post here with its height in the other pictures.

As expected, a drop in the lens has raised the image on the film. As expected also, lens movement has affected the space relationship between cube and post. Now the post top appears to have moved above the front edge of the cube, whereas in the previous picture it dropped below.

The Four Camera Movements: 2 | Shift

Shift is a sideways movement of either the front or the back of the camera. Not all view cameras provide it because its function is actually the same as rise or fall: one needs only to lay the camera on its side and raise or drop the back. Presto, there is back-shift!

The reason that rise and shift are the same is that neither changes the angle between the planes of film, lens and object. And this is important enough to bear repeating: there is no change in the *plane* of film or lens, only in its *position*. Raise or shift the back of the camera, and the film is still squarely facing the lens; the only difference is that a different part of the film is now directly behind the lens.

Since shift is simply a sideways version of rise and fall, the reader should have no trouble in figuring out its effects. They are: Back movement to the left moves the image to the left on the film. Back movement to the right moves it to the right. Left or right lens movements have just the opposite results. Image shape does not change with back-shift, but does change slightly with front-shift.

But, again in common with rise and fall, shift of the lens does affect the spatial relationship of objects, because the lens is now viewing them from a different point. The examples at right illustrate these principles, with the reference cube included for comparison.

reference cube

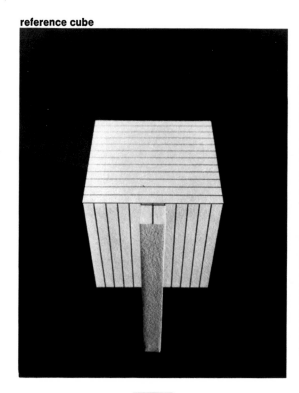

To help establish the point that shift, like rise and fall, has no perceptible effect on the shape of an object, the reference cube is repeated here. Compare it with the four cubes to the right of it. It is clear that while they have been moved back and forth on the film, they continue to look the same.

back-shift to the left

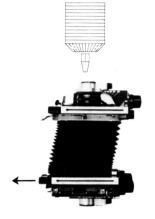

A camera equipped with a back that can move the film from side to side, as well as up and down, can place an object wherever desired on a sheet of film. Here a shift of the camera-back to the left moves the cube to the left on the film.

back-shift to the right

front-shift to the left

front-shift to the right

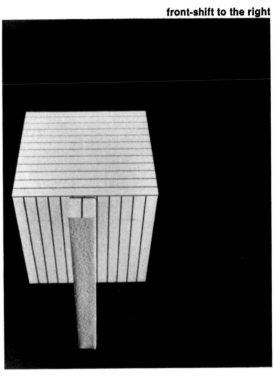

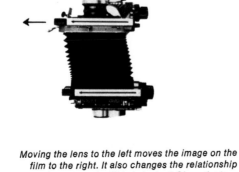

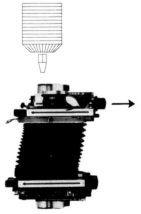

A rightward movement of the camera-back moves the image to the right. Comparison of this picture with the previous one will reveal that there has been no change in the shape of either the cube or the post in front of it. Their spatial relationship has remained unchanged also, despite the movement of the image on the film.

Moving the lens to the left moves the image on the film to the right. It also changes the relationship of post to cube. This is logical. Since the lens actually moves to left or right, it views the two objects from a slightly different position, and one object appears to have moved slightly with respect to the other. Check the position of the post against the vertical lines on the cube, in this picture and the next, to confirm this movement.

By this time it should be clear that a rightward movement of the lens, as above, (1) moves the image to the left and (2) changes the relationships in space between objects. To summarize: if you want to move the image on the film but otherwise change nothing, raise or shift the back. If you want to move the image and also change the spatial relationship of objects, do it by raising or shifting the lens—do not move the back.

151

The Four Camera Movements: 3 | Tilt

The preceding pages have shown that rise and shift have little or no effect on the shape of an object being photographed, because these movements do not change the angular relationship of the planes of film, lens and object. But what happens if the angle is changed by tilting the camera-front or -back?

Two things happen: (1) When the angle between film and lens is changed by tilting the back of the camera, the shape of the object changes. (2) When the angle between lens and object is changed by tilting the front of the camera, the focus on the object changes.

To understand why this happens, look again at the reference cube. In that picture the bottom of the film sheet was the same distance from the lens as the top of the film sheet. As a result, light rays coming from the lens to the top and the bottom of the film traveled the same distance, and the top back edge and the bottom front edge of the cube are the same size in the photograph. But change those distances by tilting —and the sizes change. The rule is: the farther the image travels inside the camera, the larger it gets. Since images appear upside down on film, tilting the top of the camera-back to the rear will make the bottom of the cube bigger in the photograph. All changes in size —and in shape—that are caused by back-tilt can be explained by this rule.

A front-tilt, by contrast, does not change distances inside the camera, and thus does not affect image size or shape, but it does affect focus by altering the lens's focal plane. Tilting the lens will bring the focal plane more nearly into parallel with one cube face or the other and thereby will improve the focus on that face.

reference cube

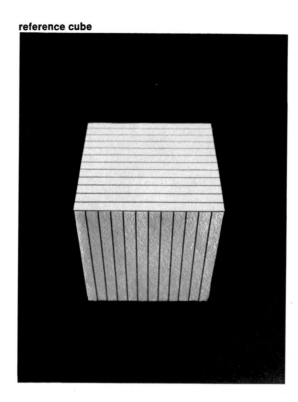

Checking the reference cube again, note that the 45° angle of view has produced an image that falls off in both size and sharpness at an equal rate on both the top and the front faces. As a result the two faces are exactly the same size and the same shape. Note also that the vertical lines on the front face are in a diminishing perspective downward; they are not parallel to one another.

back-tilt of the camera-back

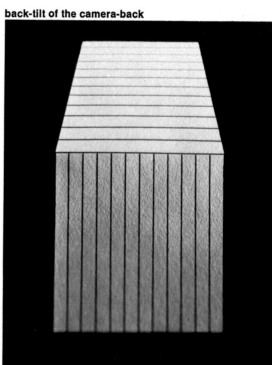

When the back of the camera is tilted so that the top of the film is farther away from the lens than in the reference shot, this movement enlarges the bottom of the cube and tends to square up its front face, bringing its lines more nearly into parallel. At the same time this tilt has moved the bottom of the film closer to the lens than it was in the reference shot, shrinking the top back edge of the cube and heightening the perspective effect.

forward-tilt of the camera-back　　　　**back-tilt of the camera-front**　　　　**forward-tilt of the camera-front**

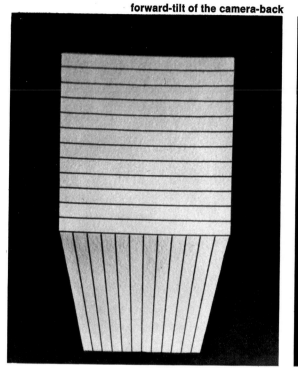

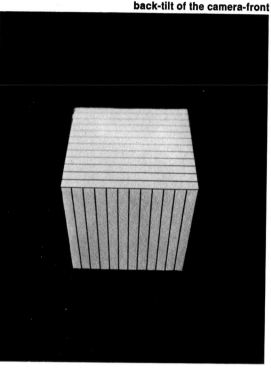

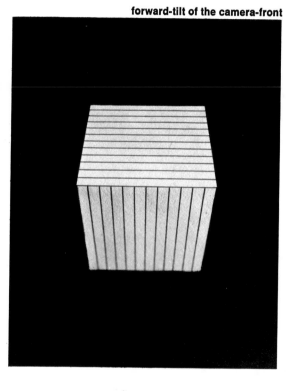

If the back of the camera is tilted the other way, so that the top of the film is forward and the bottom is moved away from the lens, the top of the cube tends to square up and the front falls into sharply diminishing perspective. Squaring up one face of the cube results in increasing light loss and increasing fuzziness toward the far edge of the squared face. In this case the back edge of the top face is so affected. In the picture at left the bottom edge of the front face is affected.

When the lens is tilted, there is no change in the distance from lens to film; thus there is no change in the shape of the cube. However, there is a change in focus. Here the lens has been tipped backward. This brings its focal plane more nearly parallel to the front face of the cube, pulling all of it into sharp focus. The top of the cube, however, is now more blurred than in the reference shot.

By tilting the lens forward, the top of the cube becomes sharp and the front more blurred. The focus control that lens-tilt gives can be put to excellent use when combined with back-tilt. Look again at the two back-tilt shots at the left; consider how much sharper their squared—and blurry—sides could have been made by tilting the lens to improve their overall focus.

The Four Camera Movements: 4 | Swing

Swing is a sideways twisting of either the front or the back of the camera around the vertical axis. Like the three movements that have been discussed so far, it has different effects, depending on whether it is the back of the camera that is being swung or the front.

A back-swing—just like a back-tilt—moves one part of the film closer to the lens while moving another part farther away. These changes in distance—again, just as in a tilt—result in changes of shape in the image.

Front-swing, since it involves swiveling the lens to left or right, skews the focal plane of the lens to one side or another. The general effect of this is to create a sharply defined zone of focus that travels at an angle across an object. A careful examination of the two right-hand cubes on the opposite page shows this. There is a narrow diagonal path of sharp focus traveling across the top of each cube and running down one side of the front.

The practical applications of the four camera movements are virtually endless. Some are subtle and complex, particularly when used in combination. Others are obvious. For example, assume that the reference cube is a house with a large garden in front of it. Raising the back of the camera *(page 148, second picture)* will raise the image on the film and permit more of the garden to be seen. Or, assume that you wish to make the reference cube resemble a very tall skyscraper viewed from above. Forward-tilt of the back *(first picture on page 153)* will give that effect. To see how swings, tilts, rises and shifts can be applied in real situations to solve specific photographic problems, see the next 15 pages.

reference cube

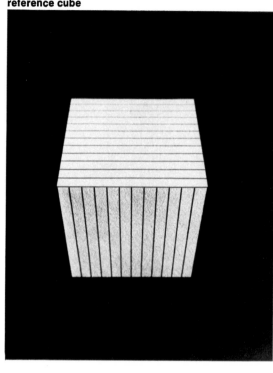

It is worth taking one last look at the reference cube to appreciate the distortions in shape that can be induced by changing the angle of film to lens. Compare the cube to the first two pictures to its right. It is hard to believe that these swing shots—or the two back-tilt shots on the previous page—are all of the same object, taken from the same spot with the same camera and lens.

left-swing of the camera-back

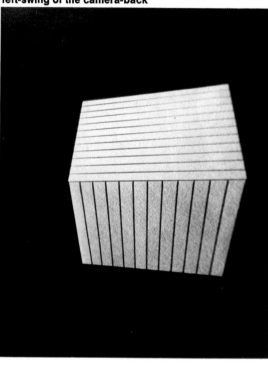

This movement of the camera-back swings the left side of the film away from the lens and the right side closer to it, making the left side of the cube smaller and the right side larger. (Remember, the image is inverted on the ground glass.) This effect is the same as tilt, but sideways instead of up and down. To grasp this better, turn this picture so that its right side becomes the top. Now it becomes an angle shot of a building, with the camera-back tilted forward to enlarge the top.

right-swing of the camera-back

left-swing of the camera-front

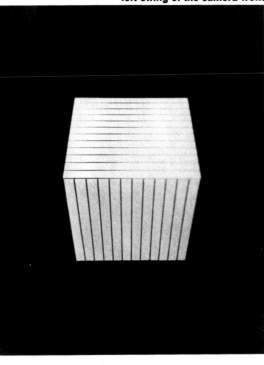

right-swing of the camera-front

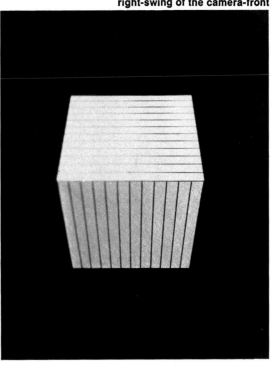

Here the right side of the film is swung away from the lens and the left side closer to it. The results are the opposite of those in the previous picture. In both of them it can be seen that there is a falling-off of sharpness on the "enlarged" corner of the cube. This can be corrected by swinging the lens or by closing down the aperture a few stops in order to increase the depth of field.

Since it is the lens that is being swung, and not the film, there is no change in the cube's shape. However, the position of the focal plane has been radically altered. In the reference shot it was parallel to the near edge of the cube, and that edge was sharp from one end to the other. Here the focus is skewed. Its plane cuts through the cube, on a course diagonally across the top and down the left side of the cube's face.

Here is the same phenomenon as in the previous picture, except that the plane of sharp focus cuts the cube along its right side instead of the left. This selectivity of focus, particularly when tilt and swing of the lens are combined, can move the focal plane around very precisely to sharpen certain objects and throw others out of focus. For a good example of this, see pages 162-163.

155

Combining Fall, Swing and Tilt to Make a Still Life

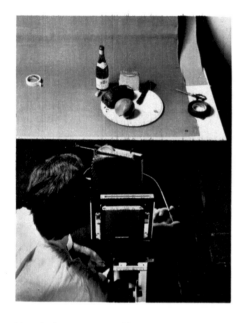

Here is the setup of Ken Kay's still life just before the final shot was made. Note the extreme right-swing of the front of the camera to get sharp focus on the bottle, the bread and the round cheese.

A still life consisting of a bottle, bread and a couple of cheeses was set up in his studio by photographer Ken Kay for a shot angled slightly downward at the arrangement. With his view camera in the right position, and with all settings at zero, Kay found several things wrong with the picture when he studied it on the ground glass of his camera. But by cranking adjustments into the camera one at a time, he was able to get an approximation of the picture he wanted. That shot *(fourth picture at right)* was, however, too far out of focus in some spots to satisfy him. Since he was working in a studio with control over his light, this was no problem. Simply by stopping his lens way down *(last picture)*, Kay was able to produce the degree of sharpness he was after.

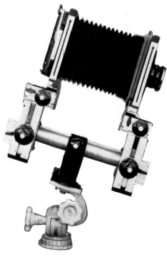

As a starter, Kay placed his camera at the desired angle with all controls set at zero. Here he is interested only in the relationship of objects: how much of the label is visible over the top of the bread, how the cut in the cheese looks, whether the cork is located properly. The setup is off center on the film, but that is of no concern as yet.

Kay's first adjustment is to bring the still life into proper position on the film. He does this with a simple fall of the camera-back. Although he plans ultimately to have the cheese in the foreground touch the bottom edge of the picture, he does not move it quite that far down at this stage because he will enlarge it with his next adjustment.

The next movement straightens up the bottle, which was leaning because of camera angle. Kay does it by back-tilt of the camera-back, using the same principle that straightened the lines on the reference cube (page 152). Back-tilt also enlarges the foreground cheese and positions it properly. But this puts some things badly out of focus.

Now Kay addresses himself to focus. Having decided that he wants the sharpest emphasis to be on the left edges of bottle, bread and foreground cheese, he swings his camera-front to the right to bring the focal plane closer to that line. Then he stops down his lens to f/22 and takes a picture that satisfies him (above right).

157

A Versatile Studio Tool: continued

Obtaining Infinite Depth of Field

One of the most common frustrations experienced by the beginning photographer comes when he tries to photograph something like a field of daisies. If he is using a camera without swings or tilts, he is in trouble. To picture the daisies properly, he has to shoot down at an angle. Obviously, the most dramatic and interesting daisies will be those closest to the camera. But if he focuses on these, the background daisies will get hopelessly blurred—and vice versa. A compromise focus—one aimed at the middle of the daisy patch—might be all right if he stopped his lens way down to increase his depth of field. But this would require a long exposure, and since daisies tend to move in the breeze during long exposures, this solution may not work.

The view camera can get around this problem. It permits sharp focus from here to infinity at maximum apertures —if a principle discovered in the 19th Century is followed. This is the fine-sounding Scheimpflug Principle, which was named after its discoverer, an otherwise obscure Austrian surveyor.

Scheimpflug hit on the fact that if the plane of the film, the plane of the lens and the plane of the subject all meet on a common line, a picture of the subject will be sharp from near edge to far. This is demonstrated by the two setups at right. In the first a wide-angle lens was used in a view camera to shoot a carpet. No tilts or swings were made. As a result, the planes of lens and film are parallel. They do not converge, and the resulting picture is not sharp overall. But by tilting the lens forward, the planes can be made to converge—and by careful focusing, a picture of dramatic overall sharpness is possible.

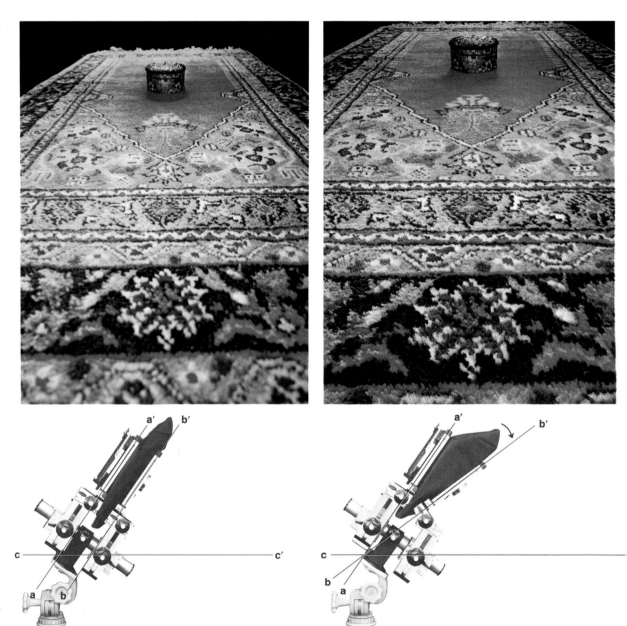

With no tilt in either back or front of the view camera, the plane of the film (line aa') cannot converge with the plane of the lens (line bb'). Therefore, they cannot meet the plane of the image (line cc') at the same point, as the diagram shows. Result, a picture that is partly out of focus.

By tilting the lens forward, its plane is changed, and now lines aa', bb' and cc' all converge, to produce a picture that is sharp overall. But the focal length of the lens was so short (65mm) that a loose bag bellows had to be substituted for the regular accordion-type bellows.

Dealing with Distortion

Every attempt to project a three-dimensional object onto a two-dimensional surface results in a distortion of one kind or another. Yet cleaning up distortion in one part of a photograph will usually induce a different kind of distortion in another. The book and orange in the two still lifes at right are examples of this. In the first picture, shot from above at a 40° angle with all camera adjustments at zero, the book shows two kinds of distortion. Since its bottom is farther away from the camera than the top, the bottom looks smaller. Also the book seems to be leaning slightly to the left. These effects would have been less pronounced if the camera had been farther away from the book —on the principle that the more distant an object is from a lens, the smaller will be the proportionate differences in distance from the lens to the center of the object and from the lens to the edge of the object. It is these differences that cause distortions in scale.

Can they be corrected? They can with a view camera, using a combination of tilts, swings and falls. Back-tilt of the camera-back straightens up the book's left edge. A left-swing of the camera-back squares up the face of the book. Fall of the back lowers the image—a necessity, since these tilts have enlarged the image somewhat.

A less distorted picture? That depends. The book is certainly squared up nicely, as if it were being looked at head on, but the spine is still visible. How can that be? Furthermore, the round orange of the first picture has now become somewhat melon-shaped. Moral: all pictures contain distortions; the photographer will have to manipulate them to suit his own taste.

With camera settings at zero, a downward view of a book makes the upper part seem larger than the lower part—just as the top-front edge of the cube on page 152 was larger than the bottom edge. This also makes the book appear to be tipping to the left. The orange, on the other hand, a sphere seen straight on in the center of the picture, exhibits no noticeable distortion.

The book is straightened up by back-tilt and left-swing of the back, but the orange is forced out of shape. These back movements also have had a bad effect on focus; it has been necessary to back-tilt the lens and swing it to the left to bring its plane into better line with the book's face.

Removing the Unwanted from a Picture

When the photograph immediately at right is studied, two awkward things become apparent about it. Both stem from the photographer's effort to get a formal, squared-up front view of a handsome Louis XV fireplace with its mirror, flanking pilasters, mantel clock and candlesticks at the Metropolitan Museum of Art in New York.

The obvious way to get such a photograph is to place the camera squarely in front of the mirror. Unfortunately a large and distracting chandelier gets in the way, blocking the top of the mirror. Worse, a reflection of the photographer and the camera can be seen. Getting around these problems with an ordinary camera requires that the picture be taken from an angle—which produces a routine shot *(second picture)* that loses the desired frontal effect. The view camera, however, can get rid of the unwanted elements and still keep the frontal effect—by using shift.

As the earlier demonstrations with the cube made clear, a shift of the camera-back to the right will move the image on the film to the right. Shift of the camera-front to the left also will move the image to the right. A combination of the two will move the right-hand portion of the image off the film and replace it with another image that could not be captured (from that position) by an ordinary camera at all.

Back to the mirror: aiming the camera straight at the wall at a point to the right of the mirror, the photographer then shifts both front and back of the camera. The planes of the camera-back, the wall and the mirror remain parallel—thus achieving the desired frontal effect with neither photographer nor camera in the picture.

A head-on shot that guarantees a squared-up picture of the fireplace and its mirror is made impossible by the chandelier hanging in the way, and also by the reflection of the photographer, who can be clearly seen in the mirror.

Moving to one side gets rid of the chandelier and the reflection, but this introduces perspective distortion into the photograph, and the squared-up head-on effect that the photographer was anxious to achieve is lost entirely.

Aiming the camera directly at the wall a little to the right of the mirror squares up everything again. Then a right-shift of the camera-back and a left-shift of the camera-front pulls the image of the mirror back into the middle of the film.

Selecting a Point of Emphasis

Often a photographer wants to emphasize only one or two things in a picture by making them sharp and letting the rest of his composition go out of focus. This is easy enough if the singled-out objects are all the same distance from the lens; he need only focus on them, open his aperture wide, and the depth of field will be so narrow that the rest of the picture will become blurred.

But what if the objects are not the same distance from the lens? Only the view camera can handle this problem. If the reader has taken in the lessons given on pages 152-155, he will know that the solution is to swing the camera lens so that its focal plane is in line with the plane of the objects he wishes to

emphasize. The two pictures opposite make this point.

The aim of the photographer was to focus sharply on a pile of beans spilling diagonally across a picture, and to let some of the surrounding jars go out of focus, keeping emphasis on the spilled beans. Since some of the beans are much nearer the lens than others, a rigid camera would have to be stopped way down in order to keep all the beans sharp. But this would bring the jars into focus too, as the top picture shows. By swinging the view camera lens and opening it wide, the photographer can create a narrow depth of field that follows the beans through the picture and leaves everything else blurred.

With camera-back and -front in zero position, a close-up shot of some spilled beans requires that the lens be stopped down to get both the foreground beans and those in the jar perfectly sharp. This also brings the other jars into focus.

A simple swing of the lens to the right brings its focal plane parallel to the receding pile of beans—all the way from the near-right foreground, back through the tipped-over jar. Now the photographer can focus on the beans and open up his lens to its maximum of f/5.6, which throws the other jars completely out of focus.

163

Changing the Look of a Skyscraper

Tall buildings are such massive structures that it is impossible to photograph them from close at hand without distortion. An ordinary street-level shot of Lever House on Park Avenue in New York, for example, would look like the first of the four pictures at right. There would be a great deal of uninteresting sidewalk, and the top of the building would be chopped off. As every amateur skyscraper-shooter knows, tipping the camera up to include the top and eliminate the sidewalk does not help. The plane of the film departs from the vertical; it is no longer parallel with the face of the building, and the resulting picture will be one of a skyscraper that seems to shrink at the top.

The second picture, taken with the camera-front raised, pulls the top of the building into the film frame and gets rid of the sidewalk. However, this gives an exaggeratedly peaked angle to the top of the building. The top-near corner seems to jut up unnaturally sharp and high. The effect can be reduced in either of two ways. The back of the camera can be swung to the left *(third picture),* which puts the film plane more nearly in line with the narrow side of the building, squaring it up somewhat. Or the back can be swung to the right *(fourth picture),* which squares up the wide side of the building. None of these last three pictures is "better" than another. Each contains its own distortion. The choice depends upon which view best serves the photographer.

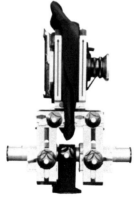

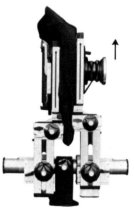

Standing at street level and shooting straight at a skyscraper produces too much street and too little building. Aiming the camera higher will not work—the lines of the building will no longer be vertical and it will seem to lean backward.

In this view, with the camera kept vertical to retain the vertical lines of the building, the roof can be pulled down into the picture by raising the camera-front. This produces an exaggeratedly sharp angle, often called the ship's-prow effect, at the top corner of the building.

A left-swing of the camera-back reduces the extremely sharp ship's-prow angle at the top of the building by placing the film plane more nearly parallel with the narrow side of the building. A left-swing of the camera-front is necessary to improve the focus on that narrow side.

Right-swings of front and back pull the wide side of the building around and further reduce the ship's-prow effect. The black areas in the upper corners of these last two pictures warn that the swings have been pushed too far; parts of the film have now been twisted so far out of line that they are outside the covering power of the lens.

Overlapping for a Wider Wide-Angle

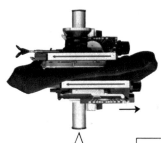

To capture wide subjects the photographer has one obvious solution: a wide-angle lens. But while such a lens will fit more of a subject into a picture, its focal length is so short that it distorts depth relationships badly, making things seem very far away. The only way to get a wide picture that also seems close to the eye of the observer *(right)* is to use a view camera with a normal lens to make two shots of the scene from the same spot. The first is made with a back-shift to the right, the second with a back-shift to the left. The two can then be fitted together to form one picture. The composite at right has a much wider field (110°) and more dramatic closeness than the single picture, above, of the same scene.

The photograph at right consists of two overlapping pictures made from the same spot by shifting the camera-back (the bracket lines at top indicate the field of view encompassed by each). The photographer also raised the camera-front when making the two pictures. In this way he was able to include more of the skyscraper than appears in the picture above, which was made with the camera settings at zero— and to get rid of the car in the foreground.

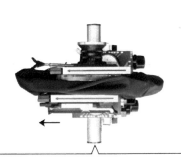

A Versatile Studio Tool: continued

The Camera as Magnifier

By general consent there are two kinds of photographs in which small things are made to seem large. There are photomacrographs, in which the enlargement is from 10 to 30 times—about the same as that provided by a strong magnifying glass. There are also photomicropraphs, in which the camera is attached to a microscope to take pictures whose enlargement is limited only by the power of the microscope.

Photomacrographs are usually made by the camera alone (without any magnifying glass or microscope attached). For their enlarging power, they depend on increasing the focal length of the lens by using extension rings or extension bellows, which put the lens at an abnormal distance from the film and thus enlarge the image. The view camera is particularly well suited to this procedure. Using large-format film, it makes pictures whose smallest details are sharp, even when blown up. Also, there are no theoretical limits to the magnification that a good view camera can deliver. Here, for example, a Sinar camera has had two additional bellows attached to it to move the film four feet away from a 16mm lens that can bring into focus objects less than an inch away. With this combination and an extra tripod to keep the whole rig steady, it is possible to magnify a single grass blade 80 times *(opposite)*. By adding another bellows or two, the enlargement could have been even greater. In either case, the view camera has become its own microscope.

An enlargement of a blade of Bahia grass was made by putting it between two sheets of laboratory glass set a half inch in front of the lens (above). There also had to be a powerful light source, since the light fall-off is very rapid on film so far from the lens. Here a 1,200-watt-second strobe light has been inserted between lens and grass. For ordinary work, this would be blindingly strong. But for this setup it gets just enough light back to the film. The photographer's assistant is shown making a test-shot with 4 x 5 Polaroid film; he has just pulled the paper from the Polaroid packet and is tripping the strobe light.

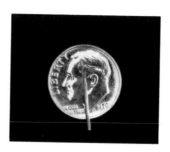

A blade of Bahia grass is shown life size above, lying on a ten-cent piece to indicate scale. At right it is magnified 80 times in a 4 x 5 photograph (reproduced here exact size) made by using three fully extended bellows on a view camera.

Creating the Illusion of Motion

A sense of movement can be imparted to a stationary object with a stationary camera—if that camera has rises and shifts. All that is required is a series of exposures on the same sheet of film, introducing a little more fall and shift with each exposure, to move the image on the film. In the picture at right, five exposures were made of a glass bird against a dark background, the back of the camera being increasingly lowered and shifted left each time. This photograph, like all the others in this chapter including the eight pages of cube demonstrations, was made by the New York photographer Ken Kay. ☐

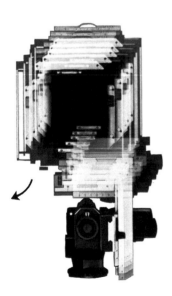

Falls and shifts, added in carefully graduated amounts for five successive exposures, produce a multiple-image shot of a glass bird that seems to swoop in a curve down through the picture. The only other help Kay gave the photograph was to dodge the bird's head to subdue its brightness. He did this with every exposure except the last.

A Room of Your Own 174

A House That Doubles as a Workshop 19

HENRY WANTLAND: *Photo Studio in Stillwater, Oklahoma,* c. 1895

A Room of Your Own

There comes a time in the life of every amateur photographer when the thought begins nagging him that perhaps he might set up his own studio. This will probably stem from a desire to work under more controlled conditions and with larger cameras than are convenient for his outside work. Still-life experiments with varying light effects, like those shown on pages 202-211, may attract him. He may be ambitious to try serious portrait work. Or he may be stimulated by the opportunities for image control that the tilts and swings of the view camera provide *(Chapter 5).*

Whatever his motivation, a day will arrive when he will catch himself looking at his basement, his back hall or his garage in a new way, and asking himself some important questions: Just what is needed to set up a studio? How much space? What about plumbing and electric circuits? Must everything be set up all at once? Or can a small, inexpensive beginning be useful?

These are among the most elusive questions in photography because the answers depend entirely on what the photographer intends to do. A studio is really nothing more than a convenience. Some of the greatest pictures ever taken were made in studios that were ludicrously primitive—not because that was the way the photographer liked it, but because that was all he had for working space, and he was able to make do with it. Apartment bathrooms, even closets to which water must be lugged in pails, have made workable—if awkward—darkrooms. The one minimum requirement is enough space to use the camera and lights effectively. Other things can be improvised, but if a man's fancy runs to full-length portraits, he cannot operate properly in an eight-foot-square bedroom, even though such space would be adequate for tabletop still-life work.

So, in terms of the pictures that are to be made, consider space first. Additional space will probably be needed for developing and printing, as well as storage for equipment and supplies. Obviously, these functions are best handled when they are located together, but they do not have to be. It is possible to do all the photography in the garage and all the processing in the basement—and get exercise walking between the two.

The space problem is often the simplest to solve. Good organization and ingenious photographic solutions permit making quite ambitious pictures in places that, at first glance, might seem totally inadequate for the purpose. There is no better illustration of this last point than the studio of Al Freni, a successful professional who conducts an active business from minuscule quarters in a midtown New York skyscraper. Although the bulk of Freni's work is close-ups for advertisers, he can also handle surprisingly large subjects, like the model with bicycle shown on page 181. Since few amateurs —and not many professionals, either—will want to attempt anything much larger than Freni's bicycle shot, the dimensions of his studio can be taken as adequate for most uses—provided the space is used as intelligently and economically as Freni uses his. The layout and equipment that get so much from so little room are worth careful study.

The space Freni occupies measures 9 by 30 feet, with an 8½-foot ceiling. With a small darkroom tucked in the back, he is left with a 22-foot-long area for taking pictures. However, not all of that is usable photographic space. There must be room at one end for seamless paper rolls—the "no-seam" used for backgrounds—to hang from the ceiling behind his subject. The subject itself often will have to be moved out into the room, several feet in front of his background, if it is to be backlit. Also, the light stands must go somewhere, which cuts down on the usable width of the room.

One way that Freni has managed to work so well in such a small space is that he has gradually accumulated a good deal of specialized photographic equipment, which increases his flexibility. What another photographer could accomplish in one way in a larger studio, Freni can manage differently in his with different props, a different camera or a special lens. This is not to say that the prospective studio-builder should make up a shopping list from what Freni uses and head for his nearest photo supplier—the bill would run to several thousand dollars. Freni himself started with two cameras, a couple of tripods, some seamless paper rolls, a table and a few lights, adding equipment as he needed it and could afford it. The reader should follow the same rule: buy nothing unless there is a specific use for it; otherwise the precious working space will shrink away little by little, and the photographer will eventually discover that he no longer has a studio but, instead, a storage room. This is a hard tendency to resist, but it should be resisted at all costs.

Freni has also saved space by putting pegboards and shelves on his walls, cupboards under all flat working surfaces. He is extremely neat. Everything has its place, and it is all carefully put away after each shooting session. He gains some additional compactness in his darkroom because it is set up to process only black-and-white film. Although he shoots a great amount of color, he finds it tricky and time-consuming to process himself, so he sends it to an outside firm.

Skimpiness in fundamental equipment, however, is false economy. An ample electric supply is, of course, a must, since some studio lights drain a good deal of power. If a 220-volt line is installed, it can be wired to supply a large number of 115-volt outlets, so that the load can be evenly distributed among them without overtaxing any one. Hot and cold running water should be available for the darkroom. In most homes the best place to find easy access to utilities—along with working space and simplicity of light-proofing —is in a basement laundry, which may even have a pair of old laundry sinks already in place, almost begging to be used to process film.

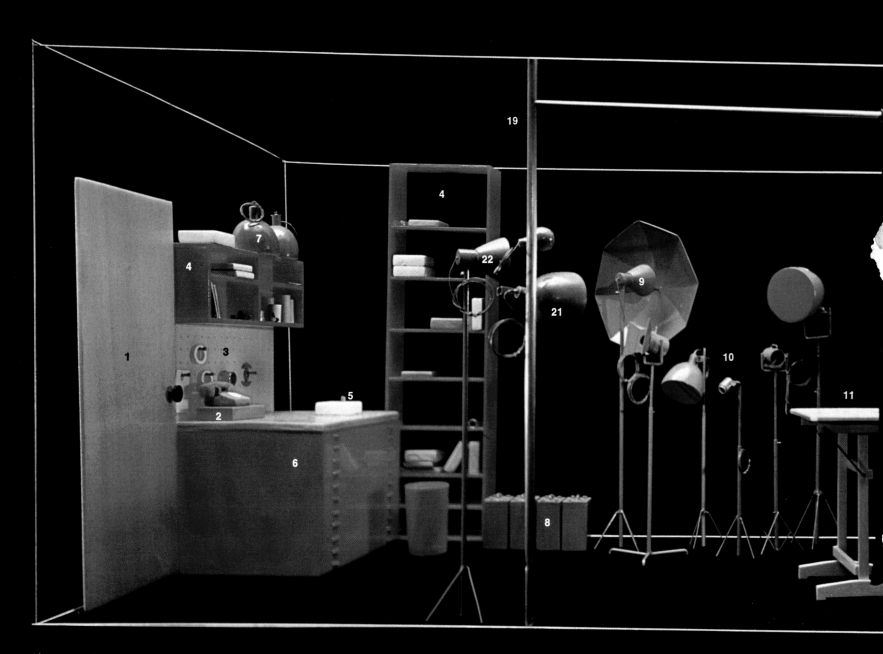

1 | entrance door
2 | telephone and telephone
answering device
3 | pegboard with tools
4 | storage shelves
5 | light box for viewing transparencies

6 | cabinet desk
7 | electronic-flash heads
and reflectors
8 | electronic-flash power packs

9 | electronic-flash
unit with umbrella
10 | flood- and spotlights
11 | table for still-life set-ups

Only 9 by 22—But a Complete Studio

In a space no larger than a one-car garage, Al Freni has set up a studio, a scale model of which is shown at left. The entrance door is at far left. Next to it is a work desk with a light box for transparencies and a telephone. Drawers are underneath. Above the desk is a pegboard for masking tape and small tools. Above that: shelves for props as well as electronic-flash heads and reflectors. More shelves are next to the desk. An assortment of some of the lights Freni needs, together with all his electronic-flash power generators, is shown in the center of the picture. The rolls of seamless paper he often uses to make plain backgrounds are stored on handmade racks under the ceiling at far right. The space underneath is not wasted—it contains filing cabinets and a print dryer.

Every studio needs adjustable surface space for setting up still-life pictures. Freni has settled on a small draftsman's table whose top can be raised, lowered or tilted. If he wants more working surface he places on the table a large square of plywood that normally stands against a wall. For still larger surface he uses the floor.

Vital to his work are three movable "pole cat" poles; their ends are under spring pressure so that they wedge themselves securely between floor and ceiling anywhere they are placed in the room. They are located where they do not interfere with photography but can be used for clamping lights or reflectors, or for suspending a seamless paper backdrop. The two poles in the foreground are connected with a horizontal rod from which drapes can be hung to provide textured backgrounds

12 | seamless paper

13 | pegboard for extension cords

14 | reflectors

15 | door to darkroom

16 | print dryer

17 | storage cabinets

18 | radio

19 | "pole cat" support poles

20 | black velvet curtain

21 | floodlight

22 | electronic-flash unit

Only 9 by 8—But a Complete Darkroom

In the model on the previous pages there is a door in the far right background. It is the same door shown here at right rear and leads to Freni's darkroom—a layout as economical of space as the studio.

The darkroom, though only nine by eight feet, is fully equipped for processing black-and-white negatives, also for making finished enlargements from them. The "wet" side for developing film and making prints is at the left in the specially constructed scale model shown opposite, with a large sink *(foreground)* that will hold two or three print trays and a wash tank. Under the sink are filing cabinet, wastebasket and storage space. Above are timers and a clothesline with pins for holding wet film and prints. Higher yet, and running all around the room, are shelves for chemicals, paper and other supplies. Along the far wall, next to the door, is a flat working surface with a paper cutter on it. Underneath are a filing cabinet and some vertical storage space. The near wall has another filing cabinet whose top Freni uses as a stand for his enlarger. The right wall is the "dry" side of the darkroom. Its flat work space has a refrigerator under it (Freni stores color film here, also ice cubes and the food products he photographs for advertising clients). Beyond the refrigerator is a lockable steel cabinet for storing cameras and lenses and an open area for hanging clothes. Air conditioning outlets are not shown; it is important that any darkroom be adequately ventilated, either by air conditioning or by fans, to dispel fumes.

1 | entrance door from studio
2 | steel cabinet with lock for equipment storage
3 | storage shelves
4 | refrigerator
5 | pegboard for tools
6 | enlarger
7 | electric timer
8 | enlarger easel
9 | storage cabinet
10 | sink
11 | print trays
12 | timer
13 | clothespins
14 | safelight
15 | folding table
16 | paper cutter

Squeezing a Big Picture into a Small Space

There are ways of making pictures that seem bigger than they are, even in small quarters. The photograph at right is a case in point. It was made by Al Freni in his studio to display knee-length sport socks.

Since the socks are sold for wear outdoors, Freni sought an outdoorsy look—so he rented a bicycle, artificial grass and some furniture. He wanted the girl's legs and the bicycle wheel to dominate his picture, and he could have done that fairly easily by using a wide-angle lens and shooting from a position close to the girl. This would have made the background props seem small and far away—as he desired —but that same wide angle would have pulled into the picture unwanted corners of the studio. A way had to be worked out to solve the background problem within walls that were only nine feet apart, and still preserve the illusion of space. To enhance this feeling of spaciousness he also wanted to make the background go just a little soft—a difficult effect to achieve with a wide-angle lens because of its great depth of field.

He solved both problems with a long-focal-length (150mm) lens on his 500C Hasselblad 2¼-inch-square camera. Its restricted depth of field slightly softened the background, and its limited angle of view eliminated the unwanted corners of the studio. All he needed now was the illusion of distance, and he achieved that by using miniature props. With a low camera angle, the table and chairs appear full size, and a respectable distance from the camera. Actually they are tiny, and only six feet behind the model, as the normal-lens shot on the opposite page reveals.

Small-scale props are the secret ingredient that gives a sense of space to a scene where space is actually missing. The table and chairs are children's garden furniture, the glasses are liqueur glasses, the "loaf" of bread a single hard roll, the bottle half the standard size. To achieve an effect of overall out-of-doors light with soft shadows, Freni bounced two electronic-flash lights off the studio walls and ceiling, and a third off an umbrella and reflecting card. The brief duration of the electronic flash's burst of light eliminated any possibility of motion blurring if his model did not hold still during the exposure.

Alternatives to the View Camera

basic 35mm equipment

optional extras for 35mm equipment

The chances are that a photographer about to set up a studio already has a 35mm camera. If so, he can make it the backbone of his studio work, adding other, larger cameras later on. Shown above is the basic equipment needed in a studio for a 35mm single-lens reflex (SLR) with a built-in light meter—with some optional extras pictured in the adjoining box at the right.

Lenses of three focal lengths are necessary: the normal 50mm lens that comes with the camera, a 28mm for wide-angle shots and great depth of field, and a 135mm for backing off to make undistorted pictures. Three filters

are recommended for black-and-white film—yellow, green and red. A cable release is needed for long exposures.

Later a second 35mm camera body with a motor drive might be bought for shooting pictures in rapid sequence. For close-up work, a set of extension rings will adapt the three lenses to making large pictures of small objects. But for extreme close-up and great sharpness of detail, a special macro lens is desirable. A zoom lens permits changing image size without having to move the camera. A valuable extra is a waist-level viewfinder—useful when the camera's viewfinder is hard to get at.

1 | **35mm SLR body with built-in light meter and 50mm f/1.4 normal lens with lens shade**
2 | **135mm f/2.8 telephoto lens**
3 | **28mm f/3.5 wide-angle lens**
4 | **filters**
5 | **cable release**
6 | **second camera body with attached motor drive and power pack**
7 | **80mm to 200mm zoom lens**
8 | **extension ring set**
9 | **55mm f/3.5 macro lens**
10 | **waist-level viewfinder**

1 | 2¼ x 2¼ SLR body with 80mm
   f/2.8 normal lens and lens shade
2 | 50mm f/4 wide-angle lens
3 | 150mm f/4 telephoto lens with lens shade
4 | filters
5 | diffusion screen for
   soft-effect portraits
6 | cable release
7 | second camera body with
   built-in motor drive, battery
   power pack, and power cord
   for recharging power pack
8 | extension ring set
9 | Polaroid back

Many studio photographers prefer a 2¼ x 2¼ camera over the 35mm for its square format and its larger film size, which simplifies the making of big, grain-free blowups. Many such cameras are twin-lens reflexes, but 2¼ x 2¼ SLRs are becoming increasingly popular; while more expensive than the twin-lens, they are also more versatile and therefore preferable for studio work.

The necessary starting lenses for a 2¼ x 2¼ are wide-angle, normal and long, as for a 35mm, but the focal lengths are different because of the difference in film size: 50mm, 80mm and 150mm respectively. Also in the kit

should be a cable release and three filters, as before. A useful new piece of basic equipment needed is a diffusion screen, its surface treated to soften the image in portrait and fashion work.

Optional extra equipment could start with extension rings for close-ups and a second motor-driven body for sequence shooting. Extremely useful too is a detachable Polaroid back, which permits the photographer to make on-the-spot test pictures of his subject before he starts shooting. If the photographer does not already have a light meter, he must get one, since it does not come built into the 2¼ x 2¼ SLR.

Two Variations of the View Camera

basic 4 x 5 equipment

optional extras for 4 x 5 equipment

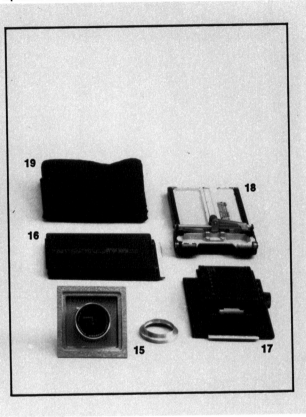

The 4 x 5 view camera is *the* studio instrument, capable of virtually complete picture control, and with a film size large enough for almost any need. The three basic lenses suggested are: wide-angle, normal and one that gives a choice of two focal lengths. The focal length for these large sizes is often measured in inches rather than in millimeters. Lenses for view cameras, like those for smaller cameras, can accept screw-on filters, but it is far less expensive to use gelatin sheets. The gelatins require filter frames, filter-frame holders and an adapter ring that fits the holder to the camera. Also needed as

basic equipment are several film holders for 4 x 5 film sheets, a cable release, a light meter and a magnifying glass for critical focusing.

Optional extras for the 4 x 5 include a large black cloth to hood the viewing screen, as an aid in focusing. Three special film holders are very handy: a Polaroid back for test shots, a 2¼ x 3¼ back that accepts the smaller, easier-to-use 120-size roll film, a 4 x 5 film-pack adapter, which holds up to 16 sheets of film together for much faster changing than is possible with single film holders. Finally, one more lens: 65mm for extreme wide-angle shots.

1 | 4 x 5 view camera body
2 | 4 x 5 cut-film holders
3 | 90mm f/6.8 wide-angle lens
4 | 150mm f/5.6 and 265mm f/12 double-focal-length lens
5 | 8½-inch f/6.3 normal lens
6 | adapter rings for lenses
7 | lens shade
8 | set of 3-inch gelatin filters
9 | adapter ring for filter-frame holder
10 | filter-frame holder

11 | filter frame
12 | studio light meter with discs for reflected and incident light
13 | magnifying glass
14 | cable release
15 | 65mm f/8 extreme-wide-angle lens and its adapter ring
16 | 4 x 5 film-pack adapter
17 | 2¼ x 3¼ roll-film holder
18 | 4 x 5 Polaroid holder
19 | focusing cloth

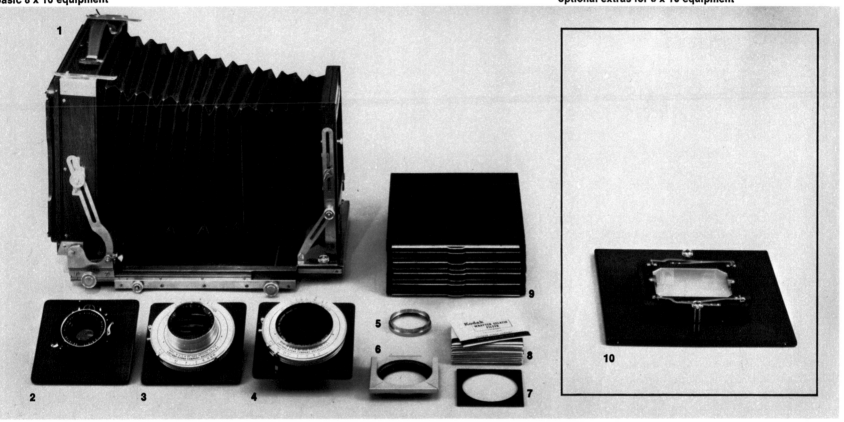

1 | **8 x 10 view camera body**
2 | **210mm f/6.8 wide-angle lens**
3 | **14-inch f/6.3 normal lens**
4 | **12-inch f/4.8 soft-focus lens**
5 | **adapter ring for 14-inch lens**
6 | **filter-frame holder**
7 | **filter frame**
8 | **set of 4-inch gelatin filters**
9 | **8 x 10 film holders**
10 | **4 x 5 revolving back**
    for film holders

For the photographer who wants to get maximum clarity and detail in his pictures by using very large film, the 8 x 10 studio camera is the answer. It can produce images four times bigger than the 4 x 5 can, but it takes up more room, it requires much heavier tripods for firm support and its film is more expensive. For these reasons it may be a less useful instrument—but, for the same reasons, it may be a very good buy. Fewer people use 8 x 10s today, and it is sometimes possible to pick up a great bargain in a used camera.

The lenses recommended as standard equipment are: a wide-angle (note that with this huge film size, wide-angle focal length has now grown to 210mm), a normal lens and a portrait lens, the latter with soft-focus properties. Also needed are 8 x 10 film holders and a set of gelatin filters, together with the same kind of filter frames and filter-frame holders that were specified for the 4 x 5 view camera, opposite.

For operating economy, a very useful extra is a 4 x 5 revolving back, which adapts the large camera to the smaller and cheaper film. It also confers another advantage: simply rotating the back allows the angling of the image on the film to any desired degree.

Tripods and Lights

The studio tripod problem is simple. The tripod will not be lugged into the field, so a good, heavy model is best. The larger tripods have extension arms that can be attached to the lower part of the center post so that cameras can be clamped to it for low-angle shots. Clamps are also useful for holding lights and reflectors.

The light problem is more complex. Cheapest and easiest to use are photofloods, which come with reflectors and stands. The floods generate heat, change the color of their light as they age and die early. A quartz floodlight is more expensive but it gives more consistent light than a photoflood of the same wattage, and lasts longer. A small spotlight is essential for highlighting particular areas. A larger spotlight has "barn doors" to keep light off surfaces where it is not wanted.

Electronic flash is still more expensive, but long-lived, heat-free and unsurpassed for stopping motion. A good studio unit should handle up to four separate lights from its power pack and deliver 300 watts to each when operating at full power. Shown opposite at lower left is a professional four-light power pack with the flash tube, reflectors and connecting cables needed for a single electronic-flash light head. An electronic-flash light meter and an umbrella reflector are also necessary. Each additional head requires the purchase of the items in the box on the opposite page, below right.

1 | extra-heavy studio tripod for 8 x 10 camera
2 | extension tube to raise head of studio tripod
3 | arm bracket for extra-heavy tripod, for low-angle shots
4 | medium-weight tripod for 4 x 5 to 8 x 10 cameras
5 | arm bracket for medium-weight tripod
6 | tripod for 35mm and 2¼ x 2¼ cameras

7 | handy clamp, small (several needed)
8 | handy clamp, medium (several needed)
9 | handy clamp, large (several needed)
10 | angle clamp, adjustable (several needed)
11 | angle clamp, plain (several needed)
12 | 3-inch "C" clamp (several needed)
13 | 5-inch "C" clamp (several needed)

1 | studio light with 12-inch
reflector and 500-watt photoflood
2 | studio light with 16-inch
reflector and 1,000-watt photoflood
3 | 1,000-watt quartz floodlight
with barn doors
4 | 200-watt spotlight
5 | 750-watt spotlight with barn doors

1 | electronic-flash power pack
with four-light capacity
2 | standard electronic-flash
head with 100° reflector
3 | protector cover for electronic
tube in flash head
4 | umbrella reflector
5 | 50° reflector
6 | extension pole to hold flash head
7 | AC power cord (top), power
synchronizer cord (center) to
connect power generator to
synchronizer cable (bottom)
that connects to camera
8 | extension cord for
electronic-flash head
9 | electronic-flash light meter
10 | second electronic-flash head
11 | second protective cover for
electronic tube in flash head
12 | second umbrella reflector
13 | second 50° reflector
14 | folding stand for second
electronic-flash head

The Darkroom Essentials

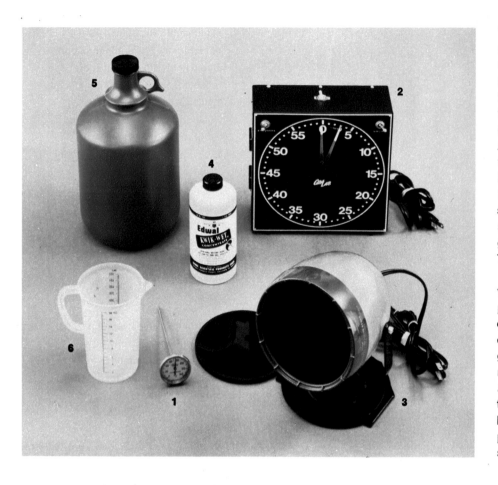

The basic darkroom shopping list includes the few standard items needed whether the film is small or large, roll or sheet, shown at left. Since film processing requires precise temperature control and timing, the list starts with a dependable thermometer and a timer. Also needed are a safelight with filters for adapting it to different film types; a bottle of wetting concentrate used in the drying of film to prevent water stains; several gallon jugs, like the one shown, for mixing chemicals, and a graduated beaker for measuring them. The chemicals are not shown.

To develop film, the photographer will need the items shown on the opposite page. He need not buy all the developing tanks shown—only those designed for the film sizes he uses, together with their respective hangers or reels. Besides, if he uses both 8 x 10 and 4 x 5 film, he can get by with only the larger tank, since his 4 x 5 film hangers will fit in it. Equipment used for printing varies widely, depending on studio needs, and is not shown. ☐

1 | thermometer
2 | electric timer, one second to one hour
3 | adjustable safelight lamp with filters
4 | wetting agent
5 | one-gallon opaque plastic jug (2 or 3 needed)
6 | 18-ounce measuring graduate

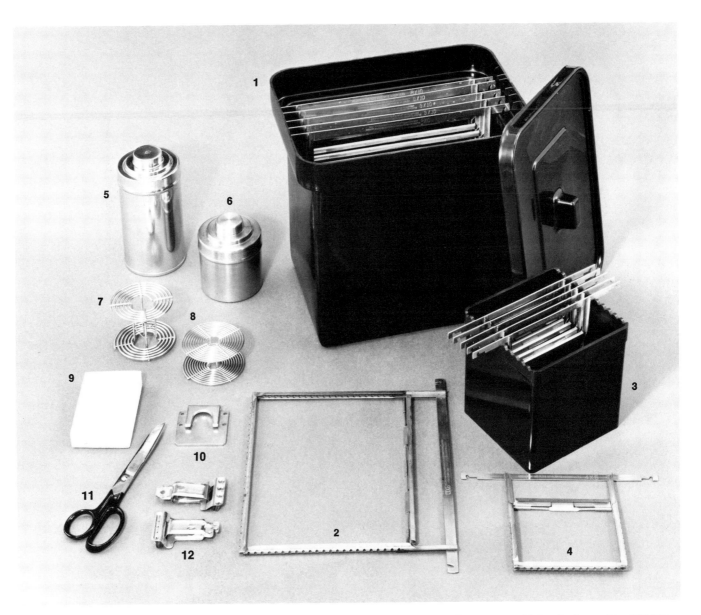

1	3½-gallon developing tank and cover for 8 x 10 film	5	large stainless-steel developing tank for roll film (holds two rolls of 120 size or four rolls of 35mm)	7	developing reel for 120 film
2	stainless-steel 8 x 10 developing hanger			8	developing reel for 35mm film
3	72-ounce developing tank for 4 x 5 film			9	sponge
4	stainless-steel 4 x 5 developing hanger	6	small stainless-steel developing tank for roll film (holds one roll of 120 or two rolls of 35mm)	10	cassette opener
				11	scissors
				12	clips for holding wet film

A House That Doubles as a Workshop

Many photographers set aside a room at home as a studio. Bob Garrett, who does general portrait work in Columbus, Georgia, carried the idea to an extreme. He turned over almost all the ground floor and garden of his home to his studio operation to provide informal, homelike settings for his portraits.

Garrett had started out in downtown Columbus with a conventional studio; then, after a decade of experience there, he began hunting for something out of the ordinary: a suburban home with a garden that he could convert into his own photographic environment. He found it after about three years of looking, a lovely house with a magnificent garden, and closed up his studio downtown to open up at home.

Both house and garden have been exploited with great skill by Garrett to provide him with a variety of backgrounds. These backgrounds help him in three ways. First, they are right at hand, always ready; no time is wasted searching them out or setting them up. Second, he has used them over and over so many times that he knows exactly how to obtain the best from any of them. Third, they are tasteful—and real; they enable his subjects to feel casually at ease, while lending a style and conviction to his pictures that would be hard to find in a conventional studio.

The lower floor of the Garrett house, at first glance, resembles any finely appointed home. Actually it is almost all studio; he, his partner-wife and one daughter live upstairs. The large front hall is discreetly given over to a reception area. At one side is a handsome sweeping staircase. Since a large part of Garrett's business is photographing brides, this staircase is an invaluable prop for a bridal pose. Elsewhere on the ground floor are French doors, fireplaces with good andirons and well-proportioned mantels, arched and pedimented doorways of several designs and sizes, two or three different wallpaper patterns. All hint of elegant and gracious living and can be worked into Garrett's pictures as he or his clients think suitable. For more straightforward portraits, he has a conventional, strobe-lit working studio room with assorted hand-painted backgrounds.

Outdoors, the Garrett studio is even more remarkable. It consists of more than an acre of garden on three levels. The ground that slopes away from the house is a maze of brick and flagstone steps, ivy-covered walls, emerald-rich patches of grass and flowering borders. An Italianate fountain springs from a formal wall and splashes into a fish pool. There is also a waterfall that trickles down over a wall of heavy rocks to a little stream that ends in a lily pond. Spaciousness is provided by a flat stretch of open lawn with a gazebo at one side and some fine old trees to give a sense of permanence. Skillful planting of holly and other evergreen shrubs makes the garden useful all the year round. Anybody—business executive, bride, matron, family group—gains a gloss of instant aristocracy by being photographed in such a setting. Just about the only thing Garrett does not provide to serve as a background prop is a live Russian wolfhound. □

Bob Garrett's Home of Photography, which he runs with his wife, daughters and sons-in-law, is headquartered in this brick Georgian house. Downstairs are seven rooms given over to photography, as are the rear gardens, which came ready-made with the house (processing is done elsewhere). The bay window and French doors shown here can be used from inside as effective backdrops for portraits.

Even the narrow hallway (far left) leading from the foyer of Garrett's house to a display corridor contributes to the homelike atmosphere of his studio. It has delicately molded arches and an English-pattern wallpaper. The viewing and salesroom (left) has a framed easel onto which an opaque projector throws proofs of portraits for examination by customers.

For a photographer with a big bridal business a dressing room (far left) is a must. Garrett has an extremely comfortable one with a three-way dressing-table mirror. He lets his sitters apply their own makeup, checking only to see that it will photograph well. The picture at left shows one of the few nonauthentic setups Garrett uses: a prop corner in his working studio, where a leather chair and fake leather books create a setting for business portraits.

A bride-to-be poses for Garrett in her wedding gown, holding a prop bouquet from a selection that he keeps on the mantelpiece in the dressing room shown on the opposite page. Below at right the bride comes out into the hall for the inevitable staircase shot, while Garrett adjusts his lights and his daughter Sandra makes the folds of the train fall exactly into place.

Garrett's garden, which he was able to put to
photographic use virtually unchanged, is rich in
good settings: at top left a grassy walk edged
with flagstones and evergreen shrubbery, at
top right a formal gazebo with brick walk and
garden table, at bottom left a graceful iron-
railed flight of brick steps that doubles around
a fountain and pool, and at bottom right a
heavy rock wall with its own little waterfall.

For an informal sylvan portrait of a family
that comes back each year to have a new picture
taken, Garrett places the group against a
background of trees in the garden's middle
level. His daughter Sandra holds an umbrella
reflector from which strobe light will be bounced
to brighten in facial shadows. Behind the group
the garden falls away into increasingly informal
settings of winding paths and a lily pond.

Overleaf: Bob Garrett's daughter Jennie poses ▶
for her own bridal portrait in front of
the waterfall at the Home of Photography.

BOB GARRETT: *Daughter Jennie as a Bride*, 1969

The Art in Everyday Objects 7

IRVING PENN: *New York Still Life with Food,* 1947

Coping with the Problems of Still Life

Many beautiful and arresting studio photographs are created from inanimate objects. Some are classic, familiar portraits—pears and wine bottles, seashells and fish—and some are abstract arrangements like matchsticks, bottle caps and paper clips. They may show one flower, one teacup, one china figurine or elaborate assemblages of almost anything from a meal set out on a kitchen table to a pile of children's toys. Ordinary household objects often make the best, and certainly the handiest, subject matter. With a bit of imagination, the photographer can transform them into fascinating pictures that transcend the everyday nature of his subjects. Irving Penn added a touch of humor and surprise to the hodgepodge of foodstuffs in his *New York Still Life with Food,* reproduced on the preceding page, by carefully pinning a beetle to the sack of dried corn.

When shooting inanimate things, the photographer enjoys a unique advantage. More than with any other kind of studio photography, he has unquestioned control over his subject. There are no live models to squirm and fidget, no chance shadows to disturb the appearance of a face or figure. Time is under his control too; he can take as long as he wants to arrange his subject and balance his lights before he trips the shutter. Such total control is also a necessity, for many ordinary objects present obstinate technical problems. How do you show the shape and indicate the volume of a wineglass, which is almost totally transparent? How do you illuminate a pottery vase so as to bring out its sheen and texture and at the same time avoid the glaring reflections from light sources? Shiny, metallic objects, such as silverware, copperware and stainless steel, have a troublesome way of mirroring things from all over the room—spotlights, tripods, cameras, furniture, even the photographer himself.

Commercial photographers face these problems daily, for many of their studio pictures are shot as advertisements for just such standard household products. To overcome the problems they use a variety of techniques and equipment. Deft use of lighting is usually the key. One obvious lighting arrangement is a pair of strong floodlights or electronic-flash units set up on either side of the subject. They will provide evenly balanced, though somewhat flat, overall illumination. To create shadows and highlights that bring out an object's shape and texture, the photographer may omit a flood and add a spotlight, or place a reflector behind the subject to backlight it and give its outline sharper definition. Another spotlight is often used for calling attention to particularly important areas of the composition. The lenses on some spotlights are adjustable, and their beams can be focused into a shaft that the photographer can aim at the exact point needed for a highlight.

But no good photographer relies exclusively on standard lighting techniques. To give himself greater control and flexibility, he shifts and varies his lights, and often turns to a number of ingenious accessories to help him adjust the shape and quality of light. By covering his light sources with diffusing material, he can soften the borderline between light and shadow. The opposite effect is accomplished by fitting lights with metal beam directors called barn doors. These devices for trimming down the beam of a spot or flood are attachments borrowed from the theater. Each pair consists of two hinged metal flaps whose name describes how they work: when the barn doors are swung wide open, the spot or flood emits a full, round flow of light. When they are partly closed, they cut off the edges of the beam, giving precise control of the area illuminated. Their principal purpose is to keep light away from places where it is not wanted: blocking it from illuminating an undesirable feature, such as a highly reflective surface, or preventing it from shining directly into the camera lens.

Other simple devices help ensure the photographer's control. Reflectors of white paper or metallic foil on a cardboard backing help him bounce light into shadowy areas. A light table, essentially a box with a translucent top, allows him to photograph his subject on an illuminating surface. He arranges the subject on the light table and places a spotlight or flood lamp underneath it, aiming the light up at the subject from below. To eliminate distracting backgrounds, the photographer often uses a sheet of seamless paper: by setting up his still life on one part of the paper and curving up the other part to form the backdrop, he eliminates the horizon line that would otherwise appear where the tabletop meets the backdrop, and gives the impression that the subject is suspended in unlimited space.

To solve the problem of unwanted reflections in shooting glassware, crockery and silverware, the photographer may shield his subject with an ingenious contraption known as a light tent *(pages 202-203, 208-209)*. It consists of an enclosure, fashioned out of white seamless paper and gauzelike fiberglass or translucent plastic sheeting, in which the subject is placed. The white paper forms the floor of the tent and usually its back; the translucent material makes up the sides and top. By aiming light through the walls of the tent, or by bouncing it around inside, the photographer surrounds the subject with diffused, glare-free illumination. At the same time, the tent blocks off any images of studio equipment that might otherwise be picked up as distracting reflections. The front of the tent is left partially uncovered to allow entry for the camera.

It takes only a bit of practice to learn how to use such versatile studio devices as barn doors and light tents. The basic principles of their application are relatively uncomplicated, and the devices themselves are almost indispensable when photographing the everyday, around-the-house articles that are chosen as the subjects of most object-photographs.

Shadows That Separate White from White

One attractive subject for the still-life photographer is the family's pure white china, but one of the most interesting ways to shoot it may be less than obvious—on a white tablecloth. Although a dark background provides a dramatic contrast, white is more subtle. Besides, a dark background may cast dull or distorting reflections.

In shooting white on white there is a risk, of course, that the china will simply disappear against the linen. The solution is in the careful use of lighting. Properly lighted, the white background can impart interesting shadows to the white cups and saucers: strong, sculptural shadows; soft, even shadows; diagonal shadow patterns that permit the simplicity of the objects to emerge. In most cases, indirect rather than direct lighting is preferable, for glare, distortion or harsh reflections are often produced by head-on illumination. On these pages Erich Hartmann has demonstrated ways to use reflected light to create striking white-on-white pictures.

Deep shadows cast by backlighting lend the photograph at left, above, a sculptural quality, bringing out the form of the cups and silhouetting the handles sharply. For this very contrasty white-on-white picture a Sungun, a high-intensity 800-watt floodlight, was directed against a white seamless-paper background (left).

The softened shadows around the cups and saucers at right, above, result from the reflection and diffusion of the Sungun's beam. To achieve this effect the cups were placed in a translucent light tent (right) and the light was aimed at the studio ceiling. The reflected light then passed through the fiberglass walls and top of the tent.

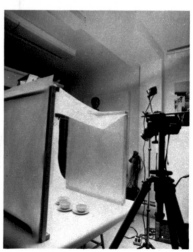

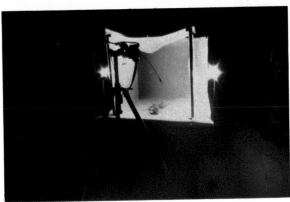

Diagonal lighting makes more obvious the hollowed shape of the cups and saucers (above, left). The slanted shadows are produced by placing two small spotlights on either side of the light tent (left). One light penetrates the tent from left center; the other is placed toward the rear. The spread of each light beam is limited by adjustable metal shields known as barn doors.

Pale, barely perceptible shadows are the only element of contrast in a photograph that shows off the purity and simplicity of the white porcelain (above). For this picture four lights were set up, as shown at right. Two small spots were trained on the light-tent ceiling; a large spotlight was angled downward onto white paper. The fourth light, the Sungun, was bounced off the studio ceiling.

Tracing the Delicacy of Glassware

Erich Hartmann approaches still-life subjects as though they were human: he tries to create studied portraits of his inanimate subjects. When he is shooting graceful glassware, for example, he seeks to bring out its inherent qualities: luminosity, transparency, sparkle. He finds that he can achieve this goal by using spotlights, which create an intense directional beam; he softens the harsh light they cast by shining them not on the glasses but on reflectors nearby. The illumination bounced off the reflectors is not softened so much that sparkle and shading are lost, but neither is it so strong that glaring hot spots or disturbing shadows are introduced. By carefully positioning reflectors and controlling the direct light reaching them with barn doors, he creates patterns of brilliance and shade that play over the glasses and the white seamless-paper background.

Halos of light tip the rims, and spots of reflection accent the bowls and bases of this overlapping series of fragile goblets. All the illumination comes from behind the glasses, thus avoiding the harsh reflections that direct frontal lighting would produce. The light was bounced off a seamless-paper background from a large spotlight (left), its beam narrowed by adjustable metal barn doors so that the reflected light would fall primarily on the lower portion of the sparkling glasses.

Light indirectly reaching the front of the wineglasses focuses attention on the delicacy of their bowls. The large spotlight facing a paper reflector screen (right) was raised high enough so that the stems cast faint diagonal shadows on the seamless paper extending beyond the glasses.

Shedding light on both foreground and background, two large spots provide a balance of illumination that defines the stemware (top) and paints the surfaces with vertical highlights.

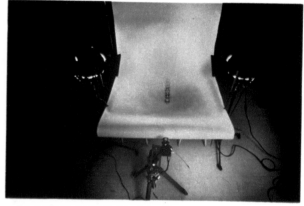

A colonnade of crystal (left) is softly backlighted by two large spotlights whose joined beams bounce off a sheet of seamless white paper, as shown above. The shadow that surrounds the bases of the glassware provides contrast with the brilliance cast by the reflected light source and lends an air of cool elegance to the photograph.

Two solid crystal figurines, a penguin and a porpoise, glow in the light of a pair of 200-watt spotlights covered with colored gelatin sheets. The spots were placed behind the translucent white seamless-paper backdrop (right), and the bright orange and blue beams they projected were narrowly confined by barn doors to bathe both penguin and porpoise in eerie hues.

The Art in Everyday Objects: *continued*
Keeping Ghosts out of the Silverware

Silver's mirrorlike qualities pose some unique problems. The highly polished pieces reflect every detail of their surroundings, a distracting trait when the surroundings include such irrelevant items as lights, photographer and camera. Sometimes reflections improve a picture, producing, as in the photograph at right, a bright and lively scene. The trick in either case is simply to move equipment around as necessary until none of it shows on the silver.

If, however, the reflective qualities of the silver must be reduced, two principal methods are available. Some photographers use matte spray, a special dulling agent that can be purchased in art-supply stores. But unless it is sparingly and cautiously used, the spray tends to produce flat, lifeless images. A better solution to the problem is a light tent like the one used for the white-on-white photographs on pages 202-203. It creates softly glowing but distraction-free pictures *(opposite).*

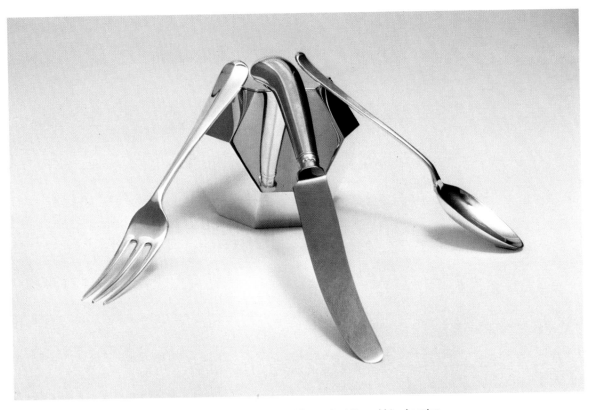

Partly enclosed in a red, white and blue housing (left), brightly polished sterling flatware and a box acquire a striped tricolor pattern (above). A brilliant Sungun floodlight was directed at the housing ceiling, subduing and scattering the light so that the silver mirrored the colors of the sides.

To minimize distracting reflections on an artful arrangement of sterling, an extra length of fiberglass was draped over the front of the photographer's light tent (right), a small opening being left for the camera lens. The subtly highlighted patterns of reflection were created by aiming the Sungun at an angled paper screen to the right of the camera. The reflected light was then diffused by the walls of the tent.

Catching the Freshness of Fruit

Each photographer develops his own favorite tricks for making fruit and vegetables glisten and appear fresh and appetizing. Some professionals use a dropper or paint brush to apply glycerine or glycerine mixtures to the food; the viscous liquid clings to the surface of the fruit and gives the impression of dewlike moisture. Alternatively, mineral oil may be applied in a thin layer to a vegetable or a piece of fruit, providing a surface on which drops of water will collect. In the center picture at right, still a third technique was employed: mist from a household spray bottle filled with water provided just the right amount of wetness.

With such tricks some form of backlighting is preferred, since it silhouettes the droplets, adding dimension to the surface texture of the fruit. The light almost always comes from electronic-flash equipment. Unlike hot floodlights, which will dry out and discolor vegetables or fruit and dissolve ice cream or aspics, the powerful flash units deliver their bursts of intense light so briefly that the food is not affected. ☐

Conveying the desired effect of moisture and freshness, juicy halves of fruit (above) glisten under light reflected from an umbrella placed over an electronic flash positioned almost directly above the subject (left). Since it shows no shadows, the black paper background concentrates attention on the rough pulpy texture of the fruit.

A close-up study of rough-textured oranges, smooth-skinned apples and a single grape (above) is enhanced by backlighted water droplets applied to the fruit with a spray bottle. An electronic flash with a fiberglass diffuser faces the fruit and its black backdrop, while another flash unit towers over the arrangement from the rear to provide the necessary backlighting (right).

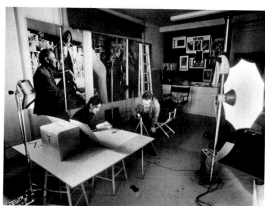

Suspended over a lemon half, a delicate, pearl-like drop of juice emphasizes the succulence of the fruit and even manages to convey a sense of tartness. The effect was created with two electronic-flash units: one, a fill-in light at the camera's left, was directed into an umbrella, and the other, partly shielded by a piece of cardboard, served as the predominating backlight.

The Professional Approach

At its best, a picture of an object is a still life in the classic sense: a work of art that, in revealing the character of the subject, arouses fresh appreciation of its qualities. This high goal is the aim of the professional studio photographer. How well he achieves it—despite unusual limitations on his artistic freedom—can be seen on these and the following pages. Only occasionally can he choose his subject matter and work with such traditional objects as flowers or fruit. More often he must create to order an image of beauty from commercial products or other objects that are infrequently associated with serious works of art—a pot, an electric lighting fixture, a piece of cloth.

To promote a line of earthenware, Henry Sandbank, a New York photographer, spent several days juxtaposing various items, searching for an austere but esthetically pleasing combination of shapes, sizes and colors. His final shot, strongly sidelighted, dramatically utilizes color, light and shadow.

The picture on the opposite page is the work of Aldo Ballo, a former architecture student who specializes in interpreting the avant-garde industrial design for which his native Milan is renowned. His photograph, commissioned by a Milanese furniture firm, clearly defines the lamp and table, but includes a pattern of reflections that makes it an effective object-portrait.

Brilliant lighting accentuates the shiny surfaces of a coffeepot and jug. A 1,000-watt flood was set to the left of the subjects while two angled pieces of white cardboard—one only slightly larger than the jug, the other slightly smaller—were placed out of camera range at the right and at the rear to guide a minimal reflection around to the right side, defining the shape of the earthenware.

HENRY SANDBANK: *Earthenware Utensils with a Spoon,* 1967

Surface sheen characterizes the red plastic of this lamp and table, illuminated from one side by two 900-watt banks of floodlights. The lamp was suspended only a foot above the tabletop in order to place it near the center of the frame, and a plate of dried fruit was so placed as to relieve the severe lines of the molded plastic objects.

ALDO BALLO: *Molded Plastic Furniture*, 1969

Fabrics in Close-up

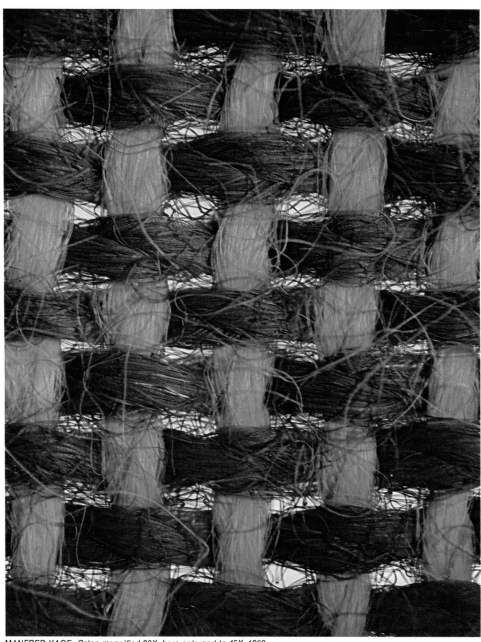

MANFRED KAGE: *Orlon magnified 20X, here enlarged to 45X, 1969*

At first glance the two pictures on these pages seem to bear no resemblance. They show different things and were made by different photographers using radically different techniques. And yet both achieve the same purpose: they convey the idea of fabric without showing fabric as it is ordinarily seen.

For the greatly enlarged view of Orlon at left, Manfred Kage set up an optical bench: a guide rail to which he attached a small lamp to backlight the fabric, a condenser lens to focus the light, a filter, the fabric sample and a view camera. The subtly colored remnants of thread in the composition at right were photographed by John Ellard in an English mill. Meticulously framing the subject with his 35mm camera, manipulating it and the lighting angle, he achieved a result as precisely controlled as Kage's.

Many times larger than life, this photomacrograph of an Orlon swatch was backlighted so that wispy dark strands of thread would be clearly visible. Frontlighting made the light-colored strands show up and revealed the pattern of the weave.

The balls of thread at right look like yarn from grandmother's knitting basket but are "thrums" —waste from the warp section of a loom. Daylight from a nearby window illuminated them.

JOHN ELLARD: *Warp Waste in a Spinning Factory,* 1969

Fine Gems in Unusual Settings

Jewelry is a most difficult subject to photograph effectively. It can be as transparent as glass and as full of reflections as silverware or cut crystal, posing a complex of problems. Small and delicate, jewelry must be photographed with utmost precision to reveal the details of workmanship. Usually it is shown in life-sized, or greater-than-life-sized, close-ups, adding to the difficulty of producing needle-sharp pictures —the closer the camera to the subject, the more restricted the depth of field and the smaller the area of sharp focus. Cut gems are particularly demanding subjects. Since their brilliance comes from the way light glints across their facets, the photographer must adjust his lighting to make as many facets glow as possible. In addition, the photographer faces the challenge of finding imaginative props to set off the jewelry's richness and elegance.

Photographers often cope with the technical difficulties of gem photography by setting up the jewels inside a light tent *(page 202),* and carefully balancing the illumination with spotlights and flood lamps. To preserve sharp focus within a limited depth of field, they usually keep the center of interest of the composition within a single plane, as in the arrangement of brooches and pendants at right. Individual photographers have discovered certain finer points of composition and lighting for themselves, and are sometimes reluctant to reveal their hard-earned formulas. Charles Collum, who made the red diamond in the coconut half glow so brilliantly on the opposite page, refuses to say exactly how he did it. "That," he declares, "would be giving away my best trade secret."

CHARLES R. COLLUM: *Arrangement with Opals,* 1969

An antique nutmeg grater provides an unusual foil for a sparkling display of opal jewelry set with cut diamonds and other gems (above). For maximum clarity, the photographer placed all the gems at the same distance from his 8 x 10 view camera. The same photographer used a coconut half to give an exotic air to his picture of a red diamond (opposite, bottom). The shaggy husk and white meat contrast with the precisely cut gem.

Fresh vegetables, according to Fred Burrell, who ▶ photographed the two brooches with tomato and artichoke slices (top right), make an ideal setting for jewelry. Fleshy, moist and alive, they set off the hardness of stone and metal. Burrell placed each vegetable, sliced paper thin, on a white translucent panel inside a light tent. Each brooch, laid on top of its vegetable slice, was lighted from below with a small spot and from above with two flood lamps and was photographed with a 4 x 5 view camera stopped down to f/22.

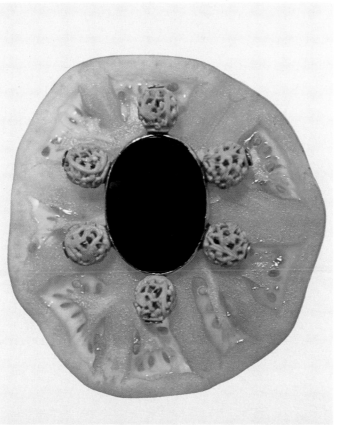

FRED BURRELL: *Brooch of Onyx and Carved Ivory*, 1968

FRED BURRELL: *Brooch of Amethysts with Jade Pendants*, 1968

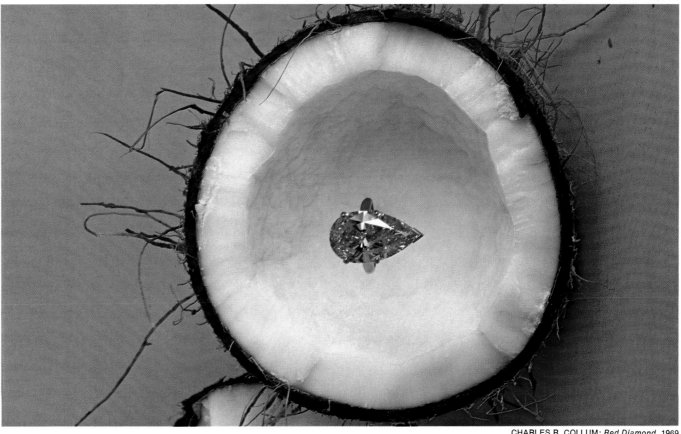

CHARLES R. COLLUM: *Red Diamond*, 1969

Liquids in Suspension

A Leitz Aristophot, an elaborate close-up apparatus, allowed the photographer to catch this strange magnified view of a blue-dyed drop of water poised near the edge of a nylon curtain. Since the curtain was water repellent, he had ample time to experiment with lighting, subject and camera angles. He placed the drop on the curtain edge, beneath the lens of the Aristophot. Two floodlights, equipped with heat-absorbing glass filters to guard against evaporation, illuminated the subject from above. A small spotlight aimed at an angled mirror below the material provided backlighting to define the sharp edges of warp, woof and water droplet.

A sleek spout of champagne, highlighted by the ▶ reflected illumination of two electronic-flash units, cascades into a pool of bubbles. The flash units, placed symmetrically on either side of the camera, were essential for stopping the motion of the pouring champagne. To eliminate shadows and distracting reflections, the photographer isolated the glass and bottle against a black velvet background. Choosing to accentuate bubbles rather than bottle in shooting this photograph for a champagne advertisement, he shielded the foil-wrapped neck of the bottle by placing pieces of cardboard between the lights and the upper part of the setup.

MANFRED KAGE: *Water Drop on a Curtain,* 1970

RETO BERNHARDT: *Advertisement for Champagne*, 1963

Bringing Toys to Life

PAUL CAPONIGRO: *Antique Dolls on a Hobbyhorse*, 1967

Daylight from a window provided just the right amount of warm light and soft shadowing to convert this photograph of heirloom dolls into a lifelike study. The careful arrangement of the dolls astride an aging hobbyhorse suggests an imminent departure into reveries of childhood.

Activity appears to pause briefly for the ▶ photographer in this old-fashioned kitchen from a 19th Century Swiss dollhouse (right). The photographer preserved the scaled perspective of the room and the detail of the miniatures by blocking off any outside reference points and by slanting a 250-watt spotlight directly into the kitchen. A 500-watt spotlight bounced off a reflecting screen below camera level helped soften the harsh shadows.

THOMAS CUGINI: *Kitchen in a Swiss Dollhouse*, 1970

The Radiance of Flowers

Flower photography is an art in itself. Every variety of blossom has its own visual personality, its own pictorial characteristics—which a good photograph can bring out. There is a kind of elegance in the convoluted petals of roses, a cheerful, down-to-earth aspect to a bunch of yellow daisies, and an imaginative photographer exploits these individual qualities when he uses flowers as subjects for still lifes.

One sensitive portrayer of nature is Paul Caponigro, who has caught on these pages the character and beauty of two flowers—a fragile thistle puff and a robust sunflower. "Things in nature radiate a being of their own," Caponigro says. And with imaginative use of available light, a 4 x 5 view camera on a tripod and a poet's discerning eye, he has managed to distill this radiance onto film.

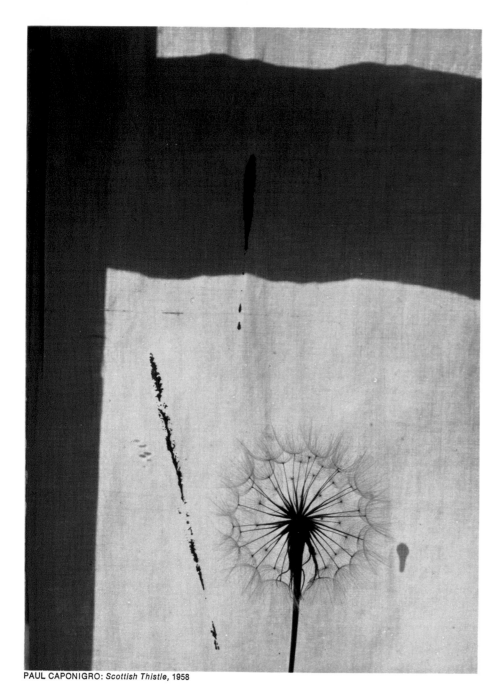

PAUL CAPONIGRO: *Scottish Thistle, 1958*

The cobweb delicacy of a Scottish thistle ready to broadcast its seeds becomes all the more apparent when shown in silhouette. "I found a paint-spattered window drape against a window with diffuse light coming through," Caponigro noted. "It made a fine background against which to place my thistle." The contrast with the massive shadow of the window sash emphasized still further the fragility of the thistle.

Strong backlighting from an open window turns this sunflower into a burst of luminous petals. The dark background was created by draping the lower half of the window with a black cloth. The light came through the unshaded upper half.

PAUL CAPONIGRO: *Sunflower*, 1965

Exploring the Beauty of Food

PAUL CAPONIGRO: *Pear,* 1964

As raw material for still lifes, food is as fascinating to studio photographers as it always has been to painters. Edward Weston became so intrigued with the involuted shapes of green peppers that he used them in numberless photographs. Edward Steichen regards a still life of three pears and an apple as one of the most successful compositions of his entire career.

Many photographers of food, like B. Trutmann, who made the picture of the fish on the opposite page, celebrate the fact that food is good to eat. They revel in the juiciness of a ripened peach or the succulence of a broiled steak. But for many others, appetizing qualities are less important than pictorial values of shape and texture. The pear at left is not something to be offered as a dessert; it is an interesting shape with a strangely mottled skin. And in the table settings on the following two pages, every object is reduced to a formal element of design.

Texture and shape, rather than edibility, are the real subjects of this pear photograph. Caponigro waited until the pear's skin had darkened, then he placed the fruit on a dark cloth and photographed it from overhead with a 4 x 5 view camera. Natural light slanting in from a window at the right provided the only illumination.

This speckle-backed pike is obviously meant to be cooked and eaten. Artfully arranged with parsley and lemon on the kind of paper fishmongers use when weighing their wares, it was photographed to illustrate an article on cooking in a French fashion magazine.

B. TRUTMANN: *Still Life with Fish*, 1965

BERT STERN: *Bread and Wine*, 1953

The ingredients of a classically simple meal —a loaf of bread and a bottle of wine—are served up as the main elements of a meticulously balanced design. The photographer arranged the bottle to complement the dark, vertical cylinder of the table base; the horizontal line of the tabletop is reinforced by the knife blade jutting in from the left. The folds of the napkin not only hide the support that keeps the knife in place, but also echo the curved shape of the bread.

The milk is as unappetizing as chalk, and the fried ▶ egg looks as hard and shiny as china, but this picture, with its strong patterns and strange perspectives, is immensely powerful. "By pure design and composition," notes the photographer, "I was able to create a surrealistic photograph using these generic food objects." He suspended his view camera above the table, but slightly ahead of its forward edge, to take the picture from an angle rather than from squarely overhead. A single spotlight was located below the camera to cast the dark shadows of the bottle and glass against the light backboard.

HENRY SANDBANK: *Egg and Milk*, 1968

PETE TURNER: *Cruets with a Lemon,* 1968

These two esthetic compositions were created from the commonest of objects, but with totally different techniques. Pete Turner arranged the one above with painstaking care: he filled a cruet with red vinegar, stoppered it tightly, upended it, and rested a lemon on its base. He then filled another cruet

with olive oil, put a sprig of tarragon in it, and suspended it above the lemon. An electronic flash, poised overhead, shone through the oil-filled cruet to deepen the yellow of the lemon; another flash, aimed at white cardboard in the background, silhouetted the fruit.

By contrast, Gene Laurents' picture

(opposite) is the result of patient observation. Living in Paris, he noticed that the proprietor of a restaurant regularly displayed fresh fruit behind an etched-glass window. Laurents kept watching until the day when the arrangement was precisely to his liking, and shot his picture at twilight to give it a purplish cast.

GENE LAURENTS: *Pears in a Paris Window*, 1961

. . . Even the Kitchen Sink

A kitchen sink? Yes, even such utilitarian hardware can be a still life, and possibly a beautiful one. Lynn St. John proves the point by artful use of lighting in this picture, made as an advertisement for kitchen plumbing.

St. John faced all the usual problems encountered when photographing reflective surfaces—in this case, chrome and enamel. He solved them by illuminating his subject with two electronic-flash units bounced off a white board placed in front of the sink at an angle of 45°. This left the foreground portion of the faucets in shadow. To give shape to the polished enamel interior of the sink, he pasted black strips onto the white board, placed to prevent light from reflecting off parts of its bottom and sides. The cool, modeled beauty of the result seems as sleek and efficient as the control console of a sports car —and as arresting as a specimen of contemporary sculpture. ☐

LYNN ST. JOHN: *Kitchen Sink*, 1967

Bibliography

Avedon, Richard, and Truman Capote, *Observations*. Simon & Schuster, 1959.

Ballard, Bettina, *In My Fashion*. David McKay, 1960.

Beaton, Cecil:
The Glass of Fashion. Doubleday, 1954.
The Wandering Years. Little, Brown, 1961.

Blum, Daniel, *A Pictorial History of the Silent Screen*. Grosset & Dunlap, 1953.

Chase, Edna Woolman, and Ilka Chase, *Always in Vogue*. Doubleday, 1954.

Giebelhausen, Joachim, ed., *Manual of Applied Photography*. Verlag Grossbild-Technik, 1966.

Horst, Horst P., *Photographs of a Decade*. J. J. Augustin, 1962.

Levin, Phyllis Lee, *The Wheels of Fashion*. Doubleday, 1965.

MacGowan, Kenneth, *Behind the Screen*. Delacorte, 1965.

Newhall, Beaumont, *The History of Photography*. The Museum of Modern Art, 1964.

Penn, Irving, *Moments Preserved*. Simon & Schuster, 1960.

Pollack, Peter, *The Picture History of Photography*. Harry N. Abrams, 1958.

Ray, Man, *Man Ray, Self Portrait*. Little, Brown, 1963.

Snow, Carmel, with Mary Louise Aswell, *The World of Carmel Snow*. McGraw-Hill, 1962.

Stroebel, Leslie, *View Camera Techniques*. Hastings House, 1967.

Taft, Robert, *Photography and the American Scene*. Dover, 1938.

Taylor, Deems, *A Pictorial History of the Movies*. Simon & Schuster, 1943.

Trahey, Jane, ed., *Harper's Bazaar, 100 Years of the American Female*. Random House, 1967.

Wahl, Paul, *Press/View Camera Technique*. American Photographic Book Publishing, 1969.

Magazines

Aperture, Aperture Inc., New York City.

British Journal of Photography, Henry Greenwood and Co., London.

Camera, C. J. Bucher Ltd., Lucerne, Switzerland.

Camera 35, U.S. Camera Publishing Co., New York City.

Creative Camera, International Federation of Amateur Photographers, London.

Harper's Bazaar, Hearst Magazines, Inc., New York City.

Holiday, The Curtis Publishing Co., Philadelphia.

Infinity, American Society of Magazine Photographers, New York City.

Modern Photography, The Billboard Publishing Co., New York City.

Popular Photography, Ziff-Davis Publishing Co., New York City.

Travel & Camera, U.S. Camera Publishing Corp., New York City.

U.S. Camera World Annual, U.S. Camera Publishing Corp., New York City.

Vogue, The Condé Nast Publications Inc., New York City.

Acknowledgments

For help in the preparation of this volume, the editors wish to thank the following individuals, collections and firms: Mehemed Fehmy Agha, Malvern, Pennsylvania; Jerry Arena, Production Manager, Color Unlimited, Inc., New York City; Richard Avedon, New York City; Paul Bonner, The Condé Nast Publications Inc., New York City; Zenja Cary, Cary Kitchens, New York City; Walter Clark, Rochester, New York; F. Van Deren Coke, Deputy Director, Eastman House, Rochester, New York; Arnold Crane, Chicago, Illinois; George Cukor, Hollywood, California; Louise Dahl-Wolfe, Frenchtown, New Jersey; Louise Effron, New York City; Bea Feitler, Art Director, *Harper's Bazaar,* New York City; Ludovico Ferraglio, Ferraglio-Newbery Associates, Inc., New York City; Al Freni, New York City; George Fry, Manager, Electronic Flash Department, Willoughby's, New York City; Stanley Glaubach, New York City; Lowell Hocking, Director, Jacksonville Museum, Jacksonville, Oregon; Max Keizerstein, Manager, Studio Equipment, Willoughby's, New York City; T. J. Le Comte, Sinar Product Manager, Ehrenreich Photo-Optical Industries, Inc., Garden City, Long Island, New York; Phyllis Lee Levin, The Condé Nast Publications Inc., New York City; Eaton S. Lothrop, Jr., Editor, *Photographic Collectors' Newsletter,* Brooklyn, New York; Yvonne McHarg, New York City; Tomas Newbery, Ferraglio-Newbery Associates, Inc., New York City; Irving Penn, New York City; Charles Reiser, Professional, Commercial and Industrial Markets Division, Eastman Kodak Company, Rochester, New York; John H. Reynolds, National News Director, University of Southern California, Los Angeles, California; Hal Siegman, General Manager, Horn/Griner Studio, New York City; Harry Warnecke, New York City.

Picture Credits
Credits from left to right are separated by semicolons, from top to bottom by dashes.

COVER: Ken Kay

Chapter 1: 11—Edward Steichen, courtesy Museum of Modern Art, New York. 20—© Karsh of Ottawa from Rapho Guillumette. 21—© Arnold Newman. 22, 23—Harris & Ewing from Gilloon Photo Agency. 24, 25—Richard Avedon, copyright © 1970 The Condé Nast Publications Inc. 26—Roddy McDowall. 27—© Barbara Morgan. From *Martha Graham,* Duell, Sloan & Pearce, 1940. 28, 29—© Philippe Halsman. 30—Melvin Sokolsky, courtesy *Harper's Bazaar.* 31—Guy Bourdin, courtesy *Harper's Bazaar.* 32—Ylla from Rapho Guillumette. 33—Norman Wightman. 34—Irving Penn, copyright © 1948 The Condé Nast Publications Inc. 35—© Toni Frissell for LIFE, courtesy Library of Congress. 36—Milton Halberstadt. 37—Nob Fukuda from Photo Trends. 38—Henry Sandbank, courtesy Wells, Rich, Greene. 39—Peter Scolamiero. 40—Ernst Haas, courtesy Volkswagen. 41—Hiro, courtesy Cowles Syndicate. 42—Lionel Freedman.

Chapter 2: 45—Courtesy Anna C. Gossner. 48, 49—Evelyn Hofer, courtesy Jacksonville Museum, Jacksonville, Oregon. 50, 51—Evelyn Hofer, courtesy Henry Ford Museum and Greenfield Village. 52—T. C. Marceau, copied by Paulus Leeser, courtesy Eastman Kodak Company. 53—Copied by Paulus Leeser, courtesy Eastman Kodak Company. 54 through 57—Culver Pictures. 58—Wilton Tifft; drawing by Herbert H. Quarmby. 59—Wilton Tifft; courtesy *Daily News.* 60, 61, 62—John Senzer. 63—Rudy Muller. 64, 65, 66—Wilton Tifft. 67—Lionel Freedman. 68—Photographs by Heinz Kluetmeier; drawing by Herbert H. Quarmby. 69—Pohlman Studios. 70 through 76—Wilton Tifft.

Chapter 3: 79—John Senzer, courtesy Horn/Griner Studio. 89—Y. R. Okamoto, courtesy Lyndon Baines Johnson Library. 90, 91—© Arnold Newman. 92—Louise Dahl-Wolfe. 93—Louise Dahl-Wolfe, courtesy *Harper's Bazaar.* 94, 95, 96—John Senzer. 97—John Senzer; Rudy Muller. 99—Keith Trumbo for Irving Penn Studios. 100—Per Boije for Irving Penn Studios. 101—Irving Penn, copyright © 1967 The Condé Nast Publications Inc. 102—Irving Penn, copyright © 1970 The Condé Nast Publications Inc.

Chapter 4: 105—Edward Steichen, courtesy Museum of Modern Art, New York. 108—Baron de Meyer, copied by Paulus Leeser from *Camera Work,* courtesy Museum of Modern Art, New York. 109—Top left, Baron de Meyer, copyright © 1921 The Condé Nast Publications Inc.—Baron de Meyer, courtesy Louise Dahl-Wolfe and George Eastman House (2). 110, 111—Edward Steichen, courtesy Museum of Modern Art, New York. 112—George Hoyningen-Huene, copyright © 1931 The Condé Nast Publications Inc., courtesy Horst. 113—George Hoyningen-Huene, copyright © The Condé Nast Publications Inc., courtesy Horst. 114—Cecil Beaton, copyright © 1934 The Condé Nast Publications Inc. 115—Cecil Beaton, copyright © 1949 The Condé Nast Publications Inc.; Cecil Beaton, copyright © 1937 The Condé Nast Publications Inc. (3). 116, 117—Man Ray, courtesy *Harper's Bazaar.* 118, 119—Martin Munkacsi, courtesy *Harper's Bazaar* and Joan Munkacsi Hammes. 120—Toni Frissell, courtesy *Harper's Bazaar* and Library of Congress. 121—Toni Frissell, copyright © 1938 The Condé Nast Publications Inc. 122, 123—Louise Dahl-Wolfe, courtesy *Harper's Bazaar.* 124—Horst. 125—Horst, copyright © 1937 The Condé Nast Publications Inc. 126, 127—Irving Penn, copyright © 1947 The Condé Nast Publications Inc.; Irving Penn, copyright © 1950 The Condé Nast Publications Inc. 128—Richard Avedon. 129—Richard Avedon, copyright © 1968 The Condé Nast Publications Inc. 131—Melvin Sokolsky, courtesy *Harper's Bazaar.* 132, 133—Hiro, courtesy *Harper's Bazaar;* Art Kane. 134, 135—Silano, courtesy *Harper's Bazaar.* 136—Alberto Rizzo, courtesy *Harper's Bazaar.* 137—Bert Stern. 138—Art Kane, copyright © 1963 The Condé Nast Publications Inc. 139—Creative Team, Ulrich & Fehlman, Zurich. 140—Alen MacWeeney.

Chapter 5: 143—Ken Kay. 145—Drawing by Nicholas Fasciano. 146 through 170—Ken Kay. 158—Caucasian design rug courtesy A. Beshar Co., New York. 160, 161—Hôtel de Varengeville, Wrightman Galleries, Metropolitan Museum of Art. 170—Bird by Lalique for Nina Ricci Parfums, courtesy Jacqueline Cochran, Inc.

Chapter 6: 173—Courtesy Robert E. Cunningham. 176 through 179—Models by Nicholas Fasciano, photographs by Neal Slavin. 180 through 189—Al Freni. 180, 181—Properties courtesy F.A.O. Schwarz and RMH International, Inc. 190 through 195—John Senzer. 196—Robert Garrett.

Chapter 7: 199—Irving Penn, copyright © 1947 The Condé Nast Publications Inc. 202 through 211—Erich Hartmann from Magnum. 202, 203—China courtesy RMH International, Inc. 207—Crystal courtesy Steuben Glass. 208, 209—Silver courtesy Tiffany & Company. 212—Henry Sandbank. 213—Aldo Ballo. 214, 215—Manfred Kage from Peter Arnold; John Ellard. 216—Charles R. Collum, courtesy Glenn Advertising for Fine Jewelers Guild. 217—Fred Burrell (2)—Charles R. Collum, courtesy Glenn Advertising for Fine Jewelers Guild. 218—Manfred Kage from Peter Arnold. 219—Reto Bernhardt, courtesy Gerstner, Gredinger & Kutter, Basel. 220, 221—Paul Caponigro; © Thomas Cugini, courtesy H. P. His, Basel. 222, 223, 224—Paul Caponigro. 225—B. Truttman, courtesy Alan Porter, *Camera Magazine,* Lucerne. 226—© 1971 Bert Stern. 227—Henry Sandbank. 228—© Pete Turner. 229—Gene Laurents. 230—Lynn St. John.

Index
Numerals in italics indicate a photograph, painting or drawing of the subject mentioned.

Printed in U.S.A.